SHARED MEMORIES

HISTORY OF NORTHAMPTONSHIRE FEDERATION OF WOMEN'S INSTITUTES 1918–2003

Joyce Haynes

First published 2009
© Joyce Haynes 2009

All rights reserved. No reproduction
permitted without the prior permission
of the publisher:

Mrs. J. Haynes,
Witney, Oxon OX28 1PA

Distributed by:
Northamptonshire Federation of Women's Institutes
WI House, 71 Park View, Moulton,
Northamptonshire NN3 7UZ

ISBN 978 0 9563786 0 6

To Tom
and all other WI husbands

Front cover: Illustration by Malvina Keech
Adapted by Charlie Haynes

Produced through MRM Associates Ltd., Reading
Typeset by CJWT Solutions, St Helens

CONTENTS

FOREWORD 4

PREFACE 5

Chapter 1 – BACKGROUND AND ORIGINS PRE-1918   7

Chapter 2 – ADVENTUROUS BEGINNINGS 1918–1920   22

Chapter 3 – CONSOLIDATION 1928–1927   40

Chapter 4 – BRANCHING OUT 1928–1935   59

Chapter 5 – THINKING GLOBALLY 1936–1944   81

Chapter 6 – TAKING TIME TO RECOVER 1945–1960   110

Chapter 7 – CHANGES GALORE! 1960–1974   137

Chapter 8 – PROMOTION 1975–1989   159

Chapter 9 – REVISED CONSTITUTION and a
        NEW CENTURY 1990–2003   191

APPENDICES   222
    County Presidents • County Chairmen • County Treasurers
    • County Secretaries • County Offices • WI Transfers •
    Sources of Information

FOREWORD

Mildred Cockram (photo courtesy of Northamptonshire Newspapers)

Within these pages will be found a valuable and historical record of life in the County of Northamptonshire as shared and enjoyed by Women's Institute members over the last eighty five years.

With the common aims of truth, tolerance, justice and friendship it will be seen that members have been able to follow these principles in many ways according to the various needs of their own communities, enjoying the many talents of their membership and in being part of a great National organisation.

Those who have been privileged to travel widely among the Institutes have gained a real appreceiation of the beauties and diversities of this elongated county.

Mildred Cockram
Federation President 1971–1991

PREFACE

Why attempt a book of this nature with at least 90 years of history – but above all WHY ME?

The first part is the easiest: why write a history? Simply because there is not in existence a comprehensive history of the WI in Northamptonshire and as the Federation is proposing to lodge all its archives with the County Records Office it seemed an appropriate time to put down on paper as much information as I could gather together.

Why me you might ask? As some explanation, having moved to Northamptonshire in 1975 and not knowing much about the county, and having now been closely connected with the WI at Federation level for 30 years I have always had to do extra homework to keep up with my colleagues. In so doing I have uncovered a great deal of information and feel it should be passed on to anyone interested, either in the WI itself, or in the social history which has helped to shape the WI as it is to-day.

The other main reason is entirely personal. I am a native of what was the old WESTMORELAND in the Lake District, which is now of course CUMBRIA, and when we moved to the Cotswolds my mother joined the WI and more often than not I went too as was the pattern in the 1940s/50s. The interesting thing from my point of view, which I found out much later, was the fact that this WI at IDBURY was the one started by the wife of J.W. Robertson Scott, who in 1925 had written the first history of the National Federation from its inception in 1915 until 1925. This book was called 'The Story of the Women's Institute movement in England and Wales' and was published by the Village Press.

Mr. Robertson Scott, who was born in Wigton, Cumberland, was the founder editor of the *Countryman*, and by a strange quirk of fate being in the right place at the right time, after leaving the

J W Robertson Scott with his wife, who was a WI member.

Editor of The Countryman – First National History *J.W. Robertson Scott, with his wife.* Story of the Women's Institutes, 1925

British Council in Grosvenor Square, London, where I worked in the Books and Periodicals Department in order to help look after my mother, Mr. Scott heard of this and asked me to type and index some of his later books.

At this time he had retired from the *Countryman* and the editorship had passed to John Cripps, son of Sir Stafford, a well known Chancellor of the Exchequer. The *Countryman* had been started and printed at Idbury Manor and the offices were at the top of the lovely old house. Mr. Robertson Scott was a larger than life Bernard Shaw who had started a Good Neighbours Scheme in the village with the motto 'Oh more than happy countryman if he but knew his good fortune'. He always believed in village life and the community spirit which enabled people to educate themselves, and so was delighted when the WI came along and started in the Village School with his wife as President. When the WI eventually suspended post Second World War my mother obtained for me the bell used at WI meetings, an item which I still treasure to-day. This bell has obviously been adapted from one such as is found in servants' quarters to summon them to their duties, and may well have come from Idbury Manor itself. My first experience of joining the WI as an adult came after we moved to Surrey and my children were safely launched into Girl Guides, Ballet, Music. etc and I could begin to have some 'me' time. I joined the newly formed Tillingbourne Valley WI, just outside Guildford. Later, when I saw an advertisement asking for help in the WI office I could not get there quickly enough. It has been my privilege to work with wonderful people and the then County Secretary, was one of these. She had been in that position for well over 30 years, was then retiring and was awarded the MBE for her work with the WI in Surrey. Most of the information she had collected through the years was committed to memory and when I took over from her for three years it was my task to try and get everything put on paper.

I learnt a great deal there and eventually took VCO training. On moving to Northamptonshire in 1975, as was the usual procedure National informed my new Federation of my address and it was left to them to contact me if they wished to do so. In common with most Counties Northamptonshire was short of members able to give time to County WI because it involves a great deal of travelling, usually alone and usually at night. However, I was fortunate to be asked to serve on the Northamptonshire Organisation sub-committee by the then chairman, Suzanne Palfreyman, and the rest really is history!

Chapter 1
BACKGROUND AND ORIGINS
PRE-1918

The 90th Anniversary of the National Federation of Women's Institutes seems a very appropriate year to be starting on a history of our own Federation here in Northamptonshire. To put our history into context, it is essential to know how the WI came into being. Imagine yourself way back in 1897, in fact in Queen Victoria's Jubilee year, though not in England but in Canada. We are in Hamilton, Ontario, where Adelaide Hoodless lived with her husband John. They had four children, two boys and two girls, but the youngest boy died before his second birthday, probably from drinking contaminated milk. Adelaide blamed herself for her baby's death and she began to campaign energetically against the selling of impure milk, and for the teaching of domestic science in schools.

As the wife of a prosperous business man she was involved in the local community. She had travelled widely and become the President of the Canadian YWCA, Treasurer of the National Council of Women and assisted in founding the Victorian Order of Nurses. Of course she was often ridiculed as a woman with wild ideas who should 'stay at home and look after her children'. Adelaide was a courageous woman with a great vision of how home economics should be taught. She started with providing homes for her YWCA girls, who were mostly unskilled, teaching them book-keeping, shorthand and dressmaking. Home-making was of paramount importance in the teaching of domestic science and she persuaded the National Council of Women to back her campaign for the introduction of Home Economics into the school curriculum. She spoke on the subject all over Ontario and was heard speaking at a Farmer's meeting at the Ontario Agricultural College at Guelph by Mr. Erland Lee. As secretary of the South Wentworth Farmers' Institute he persuaded his committee to allow Adelaide Hoodless to speak at Ladies Night and he was very much impressed with a remark she made wishing women could get information on the care and feeding of infants, in much the same way as the farmers received this on the care of calves.

This photograph of Mrs. Adelaide Hoodless, founder of the Women's Institute movement in Canada in 1897, and her family was taken in 1887.

At the end of this meeting, in thanking Adelaide, he asked how many women would attend if he called a meeting to organise a women's institute. Every woman present stood and a time was set for Mrs. Hoodless to attend a meeting and to speak.

So on 19th February 1897 this meeting took place. Quoting Bernard Hoodless, Adelaide's surviving son, he said 'it was my privilege as a boy to hitch up her favourite horse, Scotty, and drive her down to Stoney Creek He remembers the meeting in the old hall, up a rickety flight of stairs, and sitting at the back wondering what it was all about.

He soon found out because 101 women attended that first meeting and agreed to hold a further meeting the following week. Apart from Mr. Erland Lee, very few of the other men were in favour of a women's organisation, saying such things as 'oh well, let them start, it won't last long without a man to run it'.

This new institute applied to the Department of Agriculture who helped with the drafting of a constitution and byelaws. The early minutes which stated the purpose of the first institute was to educate the members in order to raise the standard of running a home and family, and they went about doing this by providing classes under six headings –

Squire's Hall, Ontario, where the first Women's Institute in the world was started on 19 February 1887.

1. Domestic economy
2. Architecture, with special reference to heat, light, sanitation and ventilation.
3. Health, embracing physiology, hygiene, callisthenics and medicine
4. Floriculture and horticulture
5. Music and art
6. Literature, education, sociology and legislation.

What an ambitious programme, and what further evidence is needed of the women's institute being an educational organisation?

By Stoney Creek's 10th birthday in 1907 there were 400 branches in Canada with 71,000 members, and by 1915 this had grown to 800 WIs. Mrs. Hoodless visited London in 1899, just two years after the formation of Stoney Creek. She came as the Canadian delegate to the International Congress of the National Council of Women. Although she was questioned about the WI in Canada it was not thought to be a possibility in England because at that time it was inconceivable that women would have any contribution to make to changing the conditions of rural life.

However, although it cannot be argued against that conditions did require change, it was cheaper to import both corn and meat rather than to buy home-grown food. Even before the war had started in 1914, prompted by the Education Act of 1902, local authorities were offering improved facilities that changed the face of towns. Streets were cleaned and lit, sanitation and water were laid on, spaces were cleared for recreation and for free libraries. Labour, through the TUC, began to

Mrs. Alfred Watt, MA, MBE, who brought the movement from Canada and founded the first Institute in Great Britain. This excellent sketch is by her son, Mr. Robin West.

take over Parliament from the Liberals and Conservatives. Although this manifested itself through improved conditions in town and urban areas, it was left to farmers through membership of the Agricultural Organisation Society, which had been founded in 1901, to organise themselves.

Mr. Nugent Harris later became secretary of this Society, and it is at one of his conferences in London in 1915 that we hear of Mrs. Alfred Watt (Madge) who apparently sat in the front row and knitted throughout. She was the daughter of a Canadian KC of Scottish descent. Her husband was in the Dominion Civil Service and when he died suddenly in 1913 she was glad to have a change and visited this country. She had obtained an MA degree. And thus with her ability and resolute spirit, and knowledge of what WIs had achieved in Canada, she hoped to get a WI movement started here.

She spared no pains in her endeavours to interest people, organisations and government departments. She did not meet with much success during these two years. However, in a similar way to

Adelaide Hoodless before her, when she had attended an all male meeting, Madge Watt introduced herself to Mr. Nugent Harris after the conference and said she wished to talk to him about Women's Institutes. He became interested enough in what she told him about WIs in Canada that he invited her to his office to talk further. He felt he had at last found what he needed by way of furthering his efforts to get together an association of women to give them a chance to express themselves. If and when they had attended joint meetings they would not get up and speak saying 'we dare not as our husbands and sons would make fun of us'.

Even with Mr. Nugent Harris's support, it still took time – and one or two more enthusiastic men – to get the new organisation started. Colonel the Hon. Stapleton Cotton was one of the governors of the Agricultural Organisation Society and Chairman of the North Wales branch. He suggested that a Welsh village would be a good place to try out the idea of a WI.

In addition to Mr. Nugent Harris and Colonel the Hon. Stapleton Cotton, there were two other men behind the idea of involving women in the running of the rural economy. One was Sir Horace Plunkett, founder of the Irish Agricultural Organisation Society, who championed the idea of women being involved as they 'made the home life of the Nation' He said women desired a social life and when they had the chance they developed it. The state of living on friendly terms with neighbours is always more central and important to the life of a woman than of a man. He formulated the policy of the Three Betters stating that men would not get very far either with BETTER business or BETTER farming, unless some BETTER living could be shown. Women could do this best, he said; in fact they alone could do it. By better living he

Colonel R.S.G. Stapleton Cotton.

meant the need to reconstitute the social and economic life of the rural community to enable it to keep pace with new ideas.

Sir Horace Plunkett was invited to speak at the first annual meeting of the North Wales Branch of the Agricultural Organisation Society by Colonel the Hon. Stapleton Cotton, who had himself done a great deal for rural areas around Anglesey. He lived at Plas Llwyn within the estate of his nephew, the fourth Marquess of Anglesey, and had established a Bacon factory, an Egg Collecting Depot, and a Bulb farm. He was also an 'exquisite' knitter, producing original designs, all of these ventures having been taken up because of his disability: he had been paralysed during a thunderstorm while serving in the Zulu War.

Another speaker was Mr. R.A. Yerburgh MP, the President of the Agricultural Organisation Society and during his speech he appealed to farmers to encourage the women's movement. A further member of the committee was Principal Sir Harry Reichel, representing the University College of North Wales, who agreed with this appeal.

Although by now many people were recommending this course of action, no-one seemed able to stimulate the various agricultural organisations into getting started. It needed something radical to achieve this and so it happened with the start of the First World War in 1914. Although history says it was anticipated that this would be over by Christmas – a period of six months – it soon became apparent that this would not happen. The challenge to help with the war effort by doing all they could to produce food proved an ideal way of getting women involved and organised. The government could recognise the value of an organisation that would harness the energies of women. In July 1915 the Board of Agricultural Education issued a report which included a reference to seeing 'an opening for the creation of women's institutes'.

At the following annual meeting of the Agricultural Organisation Society a resolution was carried to adopt the Canadian idea of WIs to suit English rural conditions and to pledge that the AOS should be responsible for the work. On 14th July 1915 the governors of the AOS acted on this resolution and set up a Women's Institute committee. Mr. Nugent Harris was authorised to engage Madge Watt as an organiser.

What happened next? I think it best to quote from Constance Davies' 'A Grain of Mustard Seed' which reports a meeting held on 18th June 1915 in Llanfairpwll, at Craig, the home of Mrs. W.E. Jones, presided over by Colonel Stapleton Cotton – 'The lecturer was Mrs Watt, from British Columbia, who gave an interesting account of the work done in that portion of the Empire, by means of the Women's Institute. It was proposed by Mrs.Wilson, seconded by another Mrs Watt, of Aber

Daventry Conservatives 59

Daventry Constituency Conservative Association

Moulton & Overstone Branch

ANNUAL DINNER

At Moulton Village Hall, Pound Lane, Moulton, NN3 7SD

Friday 6th November 2009

7.30 for 8.00pm

Guest Speaker: Roger Helmer MEP

Tickets: £20 for 3 Course meal

Raffle and Cash Bar

Dress: Smart

Blue Puffa Coat £3.00

~~Purple Cardigan~~ £5.00 Pd

2.70
4.50
―――
7.20 Paid

8.0p.
1 2 8
―――
2.08

£12.80
 1 2 8
―――
 10 5 2

The first WI in Great Britian was formed at the Anglesey village of Llanfairpwll, on 11 September 1915.

Braint,that a society of this nature be established in this village. The motion was passed unanimously.'

At an open meeting held on 11th September at Craig it was decided to form a branch of the Women's Institute and The Hon. Mrs. Stapleton Cotton was elected President, Mrs. W. E. Jones of the Craig Vice-President and Treasurer, and Mrs. Wilson of Bryn Hon. Secretary. Seven other ladies were elected to the committee. Five days later a further meeting was convened with Mrs. Madge Watt present to explain the objects of the movement. The shorter name of Llanfairpwll was decided instead of the full name of the Village **Llanfairpwllgwyngyllgogerychwyrndrobwllllantysiliogogogoch**.

Regular monthly meetings of an educational and social character were to be held on the first Tuesday of each month, at 2 pm in the room kindly lent by Mrs. Jones. The subscription would be 2s. paid in advance at the annual meeting held in January each year. New members must be proposed by an existing member and members should not be confined to the parish of Llanfairpwll.

When I have visited WIs to guide them through the necessary procedure for National AGMs I have often talked about this first WI, and have quoted its first Annual Report for 1915/1916. So again, and apologising to those members who have heard it all before, I reproduce the Report from 'A Grain of Mustard Seed': 'This institute was formed in September 1915 and was quite experimental, being the first in the United Kingdom. It has proved a great success and many others in consequence have been formed in Wales and England.

Mrs Watt, who was connected with the movement in Canada, attended our first meeting and explained the objects and the working, as well as the Rules, which we have followed as far as is consistent with the different circumstances of life in Anglesey. Our meetings have been held on a regular date every month, with occasional additions, as well as social entertainments. Many subjects have been discussed and addressed and demonstrations given, which have been followed with great interest. The chief subjects were Economical Cookery, Bread Making, Hay-box Cookery, Cheap Dinners, Fruit Bottling, Jams and Jellies.

Papers were read and discussed by the members on Women's Labour on the Land, Child Welfare, Home Economics, Autumn Gardening, The Government Poultry Scheme, and the Conserving of Fruit and Vegetables, etc.

Two lady inspectors from the Board of Agriculture and Fisheries interviewed the committee with a view to reporting on the utility of the Women's Institutes.

A War Savings Association was formed in November 1915 and has now been extended to the whole of Llanfairpwll with an amalgamated committee of the Institute members and others from outside. Up to the present 56 subscribers have joined and the contributions to the end of December 1916 amounted to over £150.

We are indebted to members and friends for the following gifts: Mrs. Jones, Craig, for the use of a room, with fires, light, etc. Colonel Cotton for £150 as a nucleus for a building fund, as well as an Oil Cooking Stove, the late Mr. S. Bostock for a handsome chiming clock, the late Mr. R.A. Yerburgh for a Fruit and Vegetable Sterilizer, and many of the members have given money, crockery, table linen, etc.

Wounded soldiers have been entertained, as well as aged women and children from the Maesgarnedd Home.

The members have been entertained at two Garden Parties, by the Hon. Mrs. Stapleton Cotton and Mrs. John Williams. These social gatherings contribute largely to the success of the Institute.

The tea and refreshment arrangements have been excellent and liberal and we shall begin the next year with a balance in hand.

We have to regret our President's illness and are glad to welcome her again amongst us. God Save the King'.

Cover of A Grain of Mustard Seed ... *'It is like a grain of mustard seed, which, when it is sown in the earth, is less than all the seeds that lie in the earth; but when it is sown, it groweth up ... and shooteth out great branches'.*

Does a great deal of this sound familiar? Over all these years so much has happened and yet the WI adheres to its core values and the format of meetings is very much the same – only the subjects have changed to keep in step with the passing years.

Perhaps I should explain the general format of a WI meeting here. There are normally three parts, the WI itself organising these in whatever way they deem appropriate for them. Firstly, there is the business section meaning the reading of the Minutes, the financial statement, and the reading of the monthly letter from the County Federation, and other correspondence. The county letter may give notices about coming events, either National or County, information about new speakers/demonstrators, and also about the county and national executives for which WI members vote. After the business there is a speaker whose subject can be anything the members choose.

The programme is drawn up at the beginning of the year and on paying her subscription every member will be given the programme for that year so that she can know what to expect. After the talk there is often a competition to be judged. If the speaker is lucky and the programme well planned it will be something to do with her subject, but as WIs prefer plenty of variety in their programmes the competitions can be wide and varied and the speaker has to be on her toes. The third section of the meeting is the social part of the programme, euphemistically called the social half hour. This may take the form of a childish game, or it may be community singing or a quiz. It does not matter as long as this part of the meeting is fun. Tea of course is organised at some point in the meeting, but usually before the social half hour To explain further the fun element at the end of the meeting it was said that if a village housewife had been up since six, had cooked two sets of breakfast for the variously employed grown up members of the family, sent the children off to school and packed their dinner for them, cooked dinner for the others and washed up afterwards, looked after the fowl, swept the house, fetched water from the pump, etc. etc. etc. then she deserved a laugh once a month.

So here we are in Wales with the first WI having been formed. Mrs. Watt continued with her work as Organiser and two more Welsh WIs were formed at Trefnant (4.10.15) and Cefn (13.10.15), still with the nation at war. I imagine this is why it took somewhat longer to get the first WI off the ground in England itself, but eventually this did happen at the end of 1915 and the beginning of 1916.

Although we need not be unduly concerned with it here, controversy still surrounds the forming of the first WI in England, the two main contestants being Singleton in Sussex and Wallisdown in Dorset. This all arises through the dates of first meetings and the dates of signing the Rules. Apparently both of them were formed at the end of 1915 with Wallisdown having met first and Singleton being listed as signing the Rules first at its Consolidation meeting. Mrs. Watt started both WIs and held various meetings in November 1915. In those days and continuing into the early twenties, as I have found from Northamptonshire formations, there were the initial Formation meetings when the WI was started by an Organiser, but their next meetings Consolidated them as a WI and it was usually at these meetings that the Rules were signed. Somewhere between the two sets of meetings confusion seems to have arisen regarding dates for these first two WIs. However, Singleton is officially listed as the first English WI, although there has been a rumour that Mrs. Watt did in fact start a WI in Lancashire before either of these two – who knows! The National Federation came into being in October 1917, by which time both the counties of Sussex and Dorset had been hard at work. They both started in September 1917, the division into East and West Sussex taking place in December 1919. The two Counties drew up their own Rules but later accepted and signed the Constitution and Rules for County Federations drawn up by National.

Mrs. Watt continued to work as Organiser for two years until 1917, when the growing responsibility of forming WIs was passed to the Board of Agriculture. The Board realised they needed to have a figurehead for the Women's Institutes, someone who would know sufficient about procedure to be able to draw up a constitution and rules, to run meetings and also to find other like-minded people suitable and willing to serve on the various committees. How fortunate then that Lady Denman was suggested. Her husband had been Governor General of Australia and her background as daughter of a press magnate meant she had an independent financial base to pursue her own activities in public life. She owned her own estate at Balcombe in Sussex and all her estate cottages had piped water and sanitation, a rare luxury in those days. At this time she was 33 and full of boundless energy. She was President of the Women's Section of the Poultry Association and had plans for promoting smallholdings. In Australia she had been actively involved in the welfare of countrywomen and in England had served on committees within the Liberal Party, thus learning committee skills. She believed strongly in the right and ability of women to conduct their own affairs.

When asked, Lady Denman took over the WI with enthusiasm, dedicated to making it an organisation that could withstand stress, strain and outside influences. In October 1917 at the first General

Meeting of the existing County Federations, the National Federation of Women's Institutes was born. At first the organisation was grant aided by the Board of Agriculture. National itself did not have an elected Executive, the WI headquarters being run by a Central Committee of Management, of which Lady Denman was the Chairman. Her first Vice-Chairman was Miss Grace Hadow. She was a don and an intellectual but nevertheless had the rare gift of understanding simple needs and aspirations. She said the WI members went around with a perpetual 'WHY?' in their minds if not on their lips. Lady Denman was the expert on procedure and Miss Hadow encouraged handicraft and horticultural interests.

Miss Grace Hadow is reported as being a woman ahead of her time. She was born in 1875 in Cirencester and won a rare scholarship to a boarding school near Stroud. She followed this by going to Truro High School from where she went to teach languages and music in Germany. Although attending Somerville College where she studied English Language and Literature she was not allowed to take exams or to receive a degree as a woman. She did, however, become President of the Women's Debating Society. An energetic and likeable academic with a great belief in education and women's rights, Grace was a pioneer of the WI movement, which she believed would help to educate countrywomen and improve conditions of country life. When Cirencester WI was established in 1916 she became its first President and quickly saw the new movement's educational and social potential. At the first meeting in London of representatives of 137 WIs she moved the resolution by which the Central Committee came into being. The following year she was elected Vice-Chairman and, with Lady Denman, was closely involved in framing the constitution. From then and until her death in 1940 Grace Hadow played a vital part in the WI and has been called its mainspring. She and Lady Denman complemented one another, both valuing new ideas and being devoted to public service. To Lady Denman's strong business sense Grace Hadow contributed enthusiasm, intellect, experience, wit and humour. In any discussion she quickly grasped essentials and expressed her views clearly and incisively. She could speak without notice on almost any subject, although when invited to lecture she prepared meticulously. She often gave lectures to groups huddled round tortoise stoves wherever there was a hall, which was usually a tin army hut. An intrepid traveller and mountaineer, she conquered the Matterhorn and a side of the Fletschorn that no woman had ever braved before. She had wide interests and enjoyed sharing them – lifelong education was her abiding passion.

Lady Denman.

Miss Grace Hadow.

The finances of the new National Federation were looked after by Miss Helena Auerbach, who lived in Surrey and who had been Hon. Treasurer of the National Union of Women's Suffrage up to 1917, and because of her experience she was able to put the monetary affairs of the organisation on a firm footing. The first constitution of the WI which had been laid down in 1919 by Lady Denman and Miss Hadow stated

> The main purpose of the Women's Institute movement is to improve and develop conditions of rural life. It seeks to give all countrywomen the opportunity of working together through the WI organisation, and of putting into practice those ideals for which it stands. For the purpose of securing and fostering the said objects the WI shall have power to provide for the fuller education of women in citizenship, in public questions both national and international, in music, drama and other cultural subjects, also to secure instruction and training in all branches of handicrafts, domestic science, health and social welfare.

The members of the first elected National Executive Committee were The Lady Denman (Chairman), Miss Grace Hadow (Vice-Chairman), Mrs. Auerbach (Surrey – Hon. Treasurer), Miss Alice Williams (Merioneth – Hon. Exhibition Organiser and Editor of *Home and Country*), Mrs Clowes (Essex), Mrs. Howard Coote (Hunts), Mrs. Drage (Carnarvon), Miss Gildea (Dorset), Mrs. Greenall (Kesteven, Lincs), the Countess Grey (Northumberland), Mrs. Hardcastle (Kesteven, Lincs), Mrs. Nugent Harris, Mrs. Huddart (East Sussex), Miss Kingsmill (Hants), Mrs. Heron Maxwell (West Kent), Lady Isabel Margesson (Worcs), Lady Petre (Essex), Mrs. G. Stobart (Durham). On becoming Chief Organiser of the National Federation Mrs. Nugent Harris retired from the committee in early 1920. Representative members on the committee were Miss Talbot, CBE and The Hon. Mrs. Alfred Lyttelton, DBE both of the Ministry of Agriculture, Mr. S. Bostock, AOS. Co-opted members were Mrs Hobbs (Oxon), Mrs. Donaldson Hudson (Salop) and Mrs. Perkins (Hants).

The National Federation was given office accommodation by the Food Production Department of the AOS at 72 Victoria Street. But when the NF received a Government Grant in 1918 it could no longer be given office accommodation. However, owing to the difficulty in finding other offices it was to be early 1921 before the move to 26 Eccleston Street, Victoria, SW1 took place.

Chapter 2
ADVENTUROUS BEGINNINGS
1918–1920

Having worked our historical way through Canada, Wales and England, we now come to our own county of Northamptonshire. A refrain that keeps coming into my mind at the start of this journey is 'This is the closest thing to crazy I have ever been' – a gentle song by Katie Melua. Although I think she meant it as a love song, perhaps it is apt as I am taking a sentimental journey and indulging my secret passion.

However, this is where the real hard work begins. I have ploughed my way through all the County Minutes Books, Year Books, Annual Reports, Scrapbooks, Photograph Albums, etc. and also through the 16 black bags and numerous containers I have used to store material during my time in Northamptonshire and I hope you will enjoy the WI history that has been gleaned from them. I have tried to produce all this information in a readable form, although on occasion I will lapse into lists of dates and events. Forgive me if this does happen, because I remember at my VCO training when I had to give a talk on a WI subject I was firmly told by the tutor I had tried to include too much information. Sadly I have not been able to use your WI contributions in their original form; they are too long and there is a great deal of repetition. Obviously you all remember the same important events. However extracts and photographs have been used.

The first recorded Minutes are dated 7th December 1918 and those attending this meeting were:

Miss Mary Hirst Simpson of Chelveston, Chelveston WI
Lady Juliet Knightley of Fawsley Hall, Badby WI
Miss Mary Bouverie JP of Delapre Abbey, Hardingstone WI
Mrs. E.C. Barker of Maidwell & Draughton WI
Apologies had been received from Mrs. Gibson, Hardingstone WI and Mrs. C.B. Fisher of Clipston WI

Although it may sound somewhat idyllic, it was reported that it was snowing gently when a group of ladies walked together over cobble stones to a meeting in Northampton. How this group of ladies came together is not recorded. Bearing in mind all the articles I have read, I think it is highly likely they may all have been linked either through the Land Army or through the Suffragette movement as it was only in 1918 that women over 30 were enfranchised. Lady Denman herself had been active in the campaign as had Grace Hadow and Helena Auerbach, all officers of the National Federation, and this may have proved the catalyst for them taking up the cause of the women's institutes in their resolve to improve the quality of life for women, particularly in rural areas. It seems probable, therefore that our own Federation Officers could have been involved in the above causes being the kind of strong-minded women needed for this, and unwittingly perhaps they also became the forerunners of the many campaigns taken up in later years by the WI.

Although the Federation was not formed during the 1914–1918 War, early records of WIs such as East Haddon which was formed in early 1918 mention knitting troop comforts. This WI was in fact personally thanked for its efforts by General Haig when visiting friends in the village. Whatever we may guess at, they were certainly all community minded and come together they did. By the time of this first meeting there were 22 WIs which had all been started by Miss Simpson, a Northamptonshire member who became a National Organiser in 1920, Mrs. Nevinson, an Area Organiser, or Mrs. Barker, who had been trained as a National Organiser in 1918 and became the Hon. Secretary of the Federation. There were two WIs which had been started by a Miss Hogg, another National Organiser whom I presume had been requested to do so by the county.

How did these ladies get around the county, either to start WIs or to attend the meetings in Northampton? Did they go on horseback, by pony and trap, by train, walking or cycling. There are reports from Hardingstone WI members that Miss Bouverie, who was their President and lived at Delapre Abbey, expected them to curtsey when she passed by in her carriage and pair with the driver and footman in attendance dressed in brown and orange livery. Lady Knightley, Northamptonshire's first President, is reported as having walked through the woods from Fawsley Hall to her WI meeting at Badby eating a picnic lunch en route and arriving at the Badby meeting place in time to preside over the meeting which was held in the afternoon.

The Organisers must have stayed overnight on many an occasion. Even when I started as a VCO In 1973 it was commonplace to go early

Miss Simpson at home in her garden with one of her dogs.

and lunch with the President, or if it was an evening meeting to go to the meeting and then accept WI hospitality overnight. One of my early memories is of having lunch with Mr. and Mrs. Godfrey Talbot before going to Sanderstead WI in the afternoon. I mention this not as a 'name-dropping' exercise, but just to show how many opportunities there are within the WI to meet so many interesting and talented people who have given of their time and energy to support their belief in the aims of the organisation. In the case of the early WIs they did invariably meet in the afternoon during daylight hours. It must have been a very difficult task to form WIs intending to unite women from all walks of life who were used to 'keeping themselves to themselves'. One lady of the manor when she heard that her vote as President would rank equally with the vote of any ordinary member wrote that she could not accept such a radical movement in her village. Another later wrote to say they had done well in recruiting members in that they had '5 ladies, 5 women and one schoolteacher', However, progress the Movement did, and the first 22 of Northamptonshire's WIs are listed below and those in bold type are still with us to-day:

1. Ashby St. Ledgers 9.11.17
2. Maidwell & Draughton 16.11.17
3. **Gt. Houghton** 17.12.17
4. West Haddon 18.12.17
5. **Guilsborough** 21.12.17
6. Stanwick 5.02.18
7. King's Cliffe 11.02.18
8. **Quinton** 15.02.18
9. **Earls Barton** 20.02.18
10. **Brigstock** 5.03.18
11. Brington 8.03.18
12. **Hardingstone** 10.03.18
13. **Welton** 12.03.18
14. Hargrave 21.03.18
15. **Wootton** 15.04.18
16. Sibbertoft 29.04.18
17. East Haddon 15.05.18
18. Sudborough 27.05.18
19. **Clipston** 30.05.18
20. **Badby & Fawsley** 31.06.18
21. Collingtree 11.07.18
22. Gayton 18

Most of these WIs were Formed and Consolidated by Miss Simpson and Mrs. Barker. As I have already indicated, early openings were recorded with two dates, that of the Formation meeting when a group of people gathered together and agreed to Form a WI, and the Consolidation date when the Rules were signed, following anything up to a year or two later.

Of these 22 WIs, the 11 who have managed to stay together for over 80 years are to be congratulated. Some of the others have Re-formed more than once and some have started again many years later as an entirely new WI. Re-forming means that as long as they started again within three years from the date of suspension they could do so and have all monies, etc. returned to them carrying on as if there had been no suspension of activities: otherwise the funds were divided equally between County and National.

During the early meetings of the county WI which seem to have taken place on a Saturday afternoon, the chair seems to have been taken by various members, obviously depending on who turned up on the day. There was no election of an Executive Committee by the members at this time and therefore no official County Chairman. It was December 1920 after the Federation had been formed that the first election took place at a Council Meeting.

The members of this early management committee would elect their own Chairman, President and Secretary The first Chairman was Miss Hirst Simpson of Chelveston, with Lady Knightley of Badby the first President. This committee dealt with items ranging from WI classes, all of which they arranged for WIs, to establishing good liaison with the WIs, i.e. advising them on Rules to be followed and organising visits. In fact, everything concerning the organisation and its members went through this committee. They undertook all the work normally given to various sub-committees in later years. Fair to say, there were only a few WIs, but to have to do all the work of organising classes and promoting rural industries as well as social events must have taken a great deal of time and effort. The first image of the Federation, therefore, is of the administration and decision making taking place on Saturdays, with WIs meeting and all other work such as Formations, taking place during the week. Mrs. Emma Mary Barker, the secretary, was a native of Yorkshire, and she was living with her farmer husband at Maidwell when the first WI nationally was launched. In 1917 she convened the first meeting in Northamptonshire at her home, and later was to be responsible, with Miss Simpson, for starting many Northamptonshire WIs. Later the Barkers moved to Moulton Lodge Farm and on Mr. Barker's death in 1938 Mrs. Barker continued to live there until she herself died in 1947.

The first Executive meeting was held in what was called the Depot, which was a room situated on the Parade, Northampton, and where it was handy for the Corn Exchange, where many members' husbands would be gathered about their business. A Rest Room was to be established in the building for the benefit of members visiting the area, much as to-day. Arrangements were put in hand, hoping that the Rest Room would be open for members in February 1919.

Permission was asked to buy brushes for getting the room cleaned and ready and to arrange for a suitable fireplace. Estimates were obtained by Miss Simpson and Mrs. Barker for painting and papering ready for consideration by Lady Knightley, Miss Bouverie and themselves on Saturday, 18th January in the Room itself; floor covering and any necessary china or furniture to be investigated. Lady Knightley would arrange for Chairs from the Duston Hospital and Miss Simpson would lend an urn. Mrs. Gibson to be asked to attend if she was well enough and to be asked to do the Catering and to see the

Food Controller about the butter order. Was it still in limited supply or maybe still rationed?

Mrs. Lloyd of Brigstock offered to send a subscription towards cups, etc. The WIs were to be written to asking for volunteers to take charge of the Rest Room on the days that it was open. There was no official newsletter at the time, all WIs having to be written to individually and by hand. Later in the year, and similarly to to-day, there were complaints about lack of visitors and WIs were asked for suggestions for ways in which to make the Rest Room more popular. The difficulties of transport must have been enormous for members because the movement, being agriculturally based, meant members travelled to town usually when their husbands were going to market to sell stock, or to buy goods. Market Days were special outings for many, but the women were very dependent on their menfolk and would have to be ready to return home once the men had finished their dealings, whether walking, by pony or trap or on horseback. Sadly the Rest Room eventually closed in December 1919 due to lack of support.

Although WIs arranged their own monthly programmes and speakers for the year, the organisation of classes was done through the County arranging what they called tours of lecturers. They could not be arranged for single WIs but several had to express a desire for a particular subject. The County organised classes for them in such subjects as soft toy making and basket making. Sometimes tutors were suggested and would travel to the WIs, but otherwise members had to travel to Northampton when they would be responsible for their own travelling expenses and the County Federation would pay their fees.

Soft Toys were made with a view to selling them to the Toy Society and shares in the Society were available for purchase. In January 1919 notice was received from National of a School for teaching Toy making to be held in Birmngham in conjunction with the Toy Society. National were prepared to pay travelling expenses for any suitable candidate but the week's board and lodging was to be paid by the County or the candidate. The setting up of village industries continued to be encouraged: Chipping Warden had a successful glove industry, Culworth made raffia dinner table mats for a London store, and Long Buckby had a needlework industry. All these enterprises welcomed private orders. However, sadly by May 1919 the Toy Society was reported to be marking time until the Autumn at least. Miss Simpson's answer was to suggest that Northamptonshire patent a special toy and so it was decided to try to find out what style of toys were required by the Education Committee for use in schools (no further news on this).

Eventually the Toy Society did wind up and it was decided to find out about investments that had been made by WIs and Executive. A Statement of Account was to be requested, and when this was received, it was agreed that the balance owing to the Federation should be shared between those taking up the shares in the first instance!

The tours of lecturers were on subjects like upholstery and chair-caning and a Mrs. Orton had spoken on Government Bills affecting Women and Children. Others were on Skin Curing and String Mat making and the making of Pouffes. Apart from these lectures, the County Council were very helpful in providing courses in dressmaking and millinery, horticulture in all its branches, poultry keeping and fruit bottling. We were especially grateful for these courses as many other County Councils were retrenching and cutting down their help to WIs.

There would seem to have been no official affiliation fees, either to National or County and both relied on subscriptions or donations. To give an indication of the amounts involved, Ashby St. Ledgers had sent £1 towards the Rest Room and Quinton 10s. 6d. as a subscription to Federation funds. Funds in hand at the end of January 1919 were £8.6.10d for the Rest Room, £4.13.2d having been spent on materials.

One WI had written asking if members who had not paid their subscription were eligible to vote at the Annual Meeting, and also whether girls, who you will probably recall left school at an early age, probably 12 or 13, and had joined the WI to learn toy making, needed to pay the full subscription. Mrs. Barker, as an organiser, was asked to attend their meeting and explain that there is only one subscription which must be paid by all!

The meeting in the Corn Exchange on 8th February 1919 with Lady Knightley in the Chair, and attended by Miss Bouverie and Mrs. Barker, reported that Mrs. Nevinson, as Area Organiser (half-time) who had been appointed by National in 1918 and was a vicar's wife, was prepared to visit WIs with a view to their being established and it was arranged that she should visit King's Cliffe on Tuesday, 11th February, Hargrave on Wednesday, 12th February with Badby and Earl's Barton both on Thursday, 13th February and possibly Hardingstone on Friday, 15th February. See what I mean about hard work.

The County, it seemed had asked National for a grant, and in response to a reply from them Miss Simpson and Mrs. Barker were to inform National of the amount the County had already raised and to ask for an appropriate grant or donation.

Funds were looking up as donations amounted to between £4 and £5, subscriptions £2.10.6d, Toy Shares and Materials £12 and Rest Room £20.

At the next meeting in the Corn Exchange on 22nd March 1919 it was reported that the WI that had experienced trouble regarding payment of subscriptions was now running quite smoothly 'under new management', Other subjects dealt with at this meeting were:

1. A request from the Public Health committee for one person to serve as a WI representative. The required person must be a working woman with a family. Three members suggested were Mrs. Ned Briggs of Hargrave, Mrs. Bird of Dodford or Mrs Rogers of Earls Barton.

2. The question of the purchase of a typewriter for the secretary was to be investigated and reported on at the next meeting. It must have taken some time to purchase this as the Minutes continued to be handwritten until at least 1939. To give you some idea of the space required to write these Minutes in a 8 x 6 ins exercise book with feint ruling I produce below one line;

arrangements for the Royal

It was in May of this year that a leaflet by Lady Denman on Procedure at Meetings was approved and it was agreed a copy should be sent to Presidents and Secretaries of each Institute. Miss Bouverie was to be delegate to a special meeting called by National on 26th July, but she reported later that very little of any value was done simply because this meeting had no powers and all propositions had to go before the National Annual General Meeting to be held in October. Nothing then was undertaken by National unless they had the approval of delegates. In June it was reported that Mrs. Watt was returning to Canada and all WIs were to be asked to contribute towards her presentation.

A National Exhibition was to be held in October 1919 and it was decided to hold a County Exhibition on 4th October preceding this and a hall was to be found. St. Giles Institute Room was deemed to be suitable and was booked for 3rd and 4th October – fee 5s. without gas! The caretaker was to be 'interviewed' with regard to teas, and notices were to be sent out to all WIs, any articles for this Exhibition first to be sent to and approved by the WI committee A sub-committee was soon to be elected and it was proposed that all powers of arrangements should be given to it and permission granted to draft a schedule. Mrs. Barker was to be Exhibition Secretary and later she was asked to be the National Exhibition Secretary at Caxton Hall. The Exhibition Programme was to be left to the committee, Executive wishing the cover to be better than that of Leicestershire (friendly rivalry between Federations). Nominations for opening were Lady Denman, Lady Exeter or Lady Lilford.

As there were still only about 30 WIs at this time I can find no report of this first Exhibition but in 1920 when the WI number had risen to 55, a Day of Competitions was held in Northampton Town Hall. This was reported as 'quite a new venture, not only for Northamptonshire but for all England, a very satisfactory outcome being a balance of £11.6.8d after all expenses paid'. Talking of competitions, at the Council Meeting that year the morning session was devoted to business and in the afternoon there was a model WI monthly meeting competition for all members, conducted by Mrs. Nugent Harris.

Voluntary County Organisers (VCOs) were appointed by National in 1918 and the first VCO school was held by Mrs. Watt in Burgess Hill, Sussex in 1918, with the edict from National that such schools 'shall be used only for instruction and no discussion shall be allowed on questions of policy or administration'. Although WIs were not generally formed in towns, undoubtedly in the early days they did try to form them and they were called WI Centres. Our nearest was at Banbury and we liaised with Oxfordshire to get this started. These Centres signed Rules which were on the same lines as WI Rules except that a Centre had as its main object, in addition to those of the ordinary WI, that of serving as a link between town and country and giving help to the surrounding WIs.

Training for VCOs has of necessity changed very much over the years. Pre VCOs the Organisers came under the Women's branch of the Board of Agriculture and at this point there was a uniform which they all wore consisting of a brown belted suit nearly ankle length, worn with a cream blouse, sometimes a tie, always finished off with a brown felt hat and leather gloves. Shoes were stoutly made and the whole appearance was academic. This has led to the misconception that VCOs wore uniform but in fact they never did. There were many stories of them sweeping imperiously into meetings with capes thrown around their shoulders, etc, but it was probably just the dress of the time. The first VCO School in Northampton was held in 1921, but in the 1920s counties were given a paper for their optional use in selecting candidates to send forward. Here are some of the questions:

1. How would you answer the question 'What is a Women's Institute'?

2. Show how the self-governing principle is maintained in (a) the WI, (b) the County Federation and (c) the National Federation.

3. What are the powers of an Institute Committee and what are its responsibilities to the Institute?

4. What do you consider the essentials of a self-governing organisation? Illustrate your remarks by reference to the Women's Institute Movement.

5. What place can a Women's Institute take in village life?

6. Give notes, under appropriate headings, for an Institute Annual Meeting and draw up a specimen agenda.

7. Draft a resolution suitable for a County Federation Council Meeting agenda. The following subjects are suggested, but candidates may choose their own – Alteration of Group System in the County; Need of Club Room in County town; Desirability of holding the County Exhibition in a different centre each year; The necessity for the County Federation to support Home and Country. Put into proper form not less than two amendments to the resolutions.

8. Explain the following terms: co-option, nomination, quorum, agenda, resolution, amendment.

9. How can an Executive Committee decentralise its work? Explain the powers and duties of sub-committees. Draw up suggested Terms of Reference for a WI Entertainments sub-committee.

You could be forgiven for thinking that these subjects are all those which a prospective VCO would expect to learn about when attending a School, but perhaps they were designed just to see how much or little the candidate knew and to organise tuition accordingly. The idea of Organisers came from Mrs. Watt's original appointment by the Agricultural Organisation Society and she was quickly followed by other appointees. In 1920 our own Miss Simpson was appointed and continued in this and other roles at National until 1945. She was one of the most active Organisers in the country and was provided with a car by National to help her round the counties. When news came through to Lady Denman many years later that Miss Simpson's WI was about to close she very quickly wrote to Northamptonshire stating that Miss Simpson's WI must never close – and it never has.

Chelveston is a very active if small group and the members are proud of their association with one of the great workers of the past. Mrs. Foulger, the present President, has loaned me extracts from a booklet on Miss Simpson by Miss Joan Wake and I think you will like to hear about her, particularly as it reflects so much of life at that time.

Miss Mary Hirst Simpson was born at Tunbridge Wells in 1871 on St. George's Day. Soon afterwards the family moved to Higham Ferrers where her father bought an old-established solicitor's practice. Mary,

Miss Mary Hirst Simpson who was provided with a car by National to help her round the counties.

always known as Pollie, was the eldest of four sons and three daughters and was taught to ride at an early age and became a fine horsewoman. She never went to school but had a governess until her early teens when she developed eye trouble. She had to remain in a darkened room for a while but when she recovered she was allowed to run wild. Although she took correspondence courses to cover the gaps in her knowledge she learnt to think for herself and to explore her surroundings. She was never bookish but had a good memory for detail and developed an independence of mind.

Her mother died when Pollie was nineteen. This made an immediate change in her life as the charge of the household fell to her and her father relied on her for many things. In later years she was the person whom all the family consulted and resorted to in their joys and sorrows. Eleven years after the death of his first wife Mr. Simpson married again. Pollie continued to sit at the head of table and carve and she and her stepmother are reported as being in complete harmony and were the dearest of friends. They lived at this time between Higham Ferrers and Irchester and Pollie hunted regularly with the

Oakley. She loved all animals, especially dogs which she bred and won many prizes at Shows with them. She was good at golf and played tennis for the county in 1898. She became a brilliant hockey player and as a skilled gardener she showed sweet peas. By 1902 two of her brothers and a sister had married so the family moved to The Old Rectory at Chelveston where Pollie made her home until after her father's death in 1921. She captained the Ladies Hockey Team at Higham Ferrers followed by Captaincy of the county team and became Hon. Secretary of the Midlands Counties Association and a member of the All England Council. Hockey was still thought to be emancipated by some but this did bring her into personal contact with exceptionally energetic women in different parts of the country who thought of her as a leader and a marked person.

When the War started she volunteered and became Assistant Secretary of the Soldiers' and Sailors' Family Association, covering a large and scattered district on a bicycle. She was later assigned to the Land Army and was appointed regional organiser. There she met Miss Meriel Talbot of the Board of Agriculture, who, as well as being Director of the Land Army, was also concerned with the beginnings of the Women's Institutes in 1915. She realised Miss Simpson's value, which was also recognised by the award of an MBE at the end of the war – in 1919. She became a regular organiser for the National Federation in 1920 when Lady Denman assured her that she need not address meetings and need not stay with people she did not know! Both conditions wore thin very quickly. She was welcomed, was loved, felt happy and made others happy. Inevitably she spoke at many meetings, and would quickly detect promise in shy women and her ardour would galvanise them to develop whatever talent was found. She was delighted to find at one WI which she was nursing because the President and Secretary had died within a fortnight, that the blacksmith's wife was giving a talk on the uses of iron, and on another occasion the shepherd's wife was talking on what could be seen in the fields early in the morning in the lambing season.

In answer to her question to members at another meeting 'What is the first thing you do when you receive a letter from Headquarters?' nothing was forthcoming so she merely said in her sonorous voice 'read it'. Our variation on that nowadays is to say 'take it out of the envelope'. You will be surprised at the number of secretaries who still arrive at WI meetings and laboriously go through correspondence by taking one letter after another out of its envelope. Excuses for not being delegates have always existed and then it was 'I live a mile from a bus

The National Federation of
WOMEN'S INSTITUTES

(Established in conjunction with the Women's Branch, Food Production Department, 26 ECCLESTON STREET, 72, Victoria Street, London, S.W.1.) LONDON, S.W.1

Try what an Institute can do in your Village.

It will promote united action among existing organisations and co-ordinate and strengthen their activities.

Women's Institutes are non-sectarian and non-party and are open to all country women.

WHAT IS A WOMEN'S INSTITUTE?

A group of country women who meet at regular intervals for mutual help and friendly intercourse.

WHO RUNS THE INSTITUTE?

The members themselves.

HOW DO THE MEMBERS DERIVE BENEFIT FROM AN INSTITUTE?

They meet together once a month to exchange ideas, and from time to time invite those having practical knowledge to speak on subjects of interest.

They study how to increase the home-grown food supply and how to use it to the best advantage.

They consider national questions such as Rural Education and Housing.

They encourage Village Industries. They learn to make baskets, toys, mats, or any articles that local resources permit.

They make the Institute the centre of Social Life in the Village.

They learn the value of co-operative effort.

A MEETING WILL BE HELD TO DISCUSS THE DESIRABILITY OF FORMING A WOMEN'S INSTITUTE

IN THIS VILLAGE, _Chelveston_

IN THE _School_

AT _7.30_ O'CLOCK, ON _Friday 4th May 6th_

SPEAKER: _Mr H Simpson_

F.W.I.,4

Templar Printing Works, Birmingham.

Chelveston WI – early publicity leaflet used by Miss Simpson.

stop' or something similar whereupon Miss Simpson is said to have jumped up saying 'Have the countrywomen of ………………….. lost the use of their legs?

She had an endless fund of good stories and loved people with a sense of humour. She liked good food and particularly soggy cakes!

Her special subjects for WI members were finance and the social side of their meetings. She could always convince inexperienced and incredulous village women that it was necessary to have a county and national organisation and that it was worth paying for. She widened their outlook and roused merry laughter at meetings with her gift of acting and at one WI Conference is said to have brought the house down by acting Nero fiddling while Rome was burning wearing a pillow slip with ivy wreaths and fiddling with a poker on a turkey's wing.

Towards the end of 1921 she drafted a model syllabus for schools of WI officers and for four years ran schools in the Midlands area. It was during this period that there was great consolidation of the organisation with very rapid growth.

In 1925 she was appointed agricultural organiser having studied agriculture and horticulture seriously. When Moulton Farm Institute was established her father was closely concerned. On becoming agricultural organiser to the NFWI , the Executive were hoping to promote the teaching of food production but there was not sufficient support at this time to make it an advisable policy. Miss Simpson kept her eye on the practical needs of the country housewife and she began to judge at agricultural shows. She retired from active involvement in 1945. Lady Denman wrote of her at this time 'We shall always remember her with affection and gratitude. By her gallant work and devotion to the Institutes she has made a very special place for herself in the history of the organisation. On her retirement the feeling of gratitude was attested by the presentation of an illuminated address from 50 county federations and long lists of individual institutes.

She died in October 1947, and Lady Cynthia Spencer, who was County President at the time, said 'she was so pointful and amusing too and nobody seemed to mind she came to the Executive in Northampton with her little dog in her arms. She could reprove without hurting, and when somebody told her how pressed for time they were and how dreadfully busy she replied ' we all have the same 24 hours in our daily lives' She loved country people and country ways. I am sure her faith in them brought out the best in them I am sure, too, we owe her a great debt of gratitude in our County Federation and I hope she will never be forgotten'.

Miss Alice Williams and Mrs. Nugent Harris.

To make sure the name of Miss Simpson is never forgotten is one of the aim's of this book and to this end I feel the whole exercise is about Communication. Unless we are told about our predecessors and the WI activities of previous years how can we be expected to know all we should about the WI in Northamptonshire. And how, too, can we make sure we are all working together. This has been one of my themes during my time as a VCO and later as County Chairman, but perhaps it was even more vital in the early days and that is why it is interesting to note that the National Magazine Home and Country had its beginnings in March 1919. Miss Alice Williams was the National Treasurer and she undertook this task with the help of Mrs. Nugent Harris. The first copy consisted of 8 pages with a photograph on the front showing the first National Exhibition at Caxton Hall in October

HOME AND COUNTRY.

THE WOMEN'S INSTITUTES JOURNAL.

PUBLISHED BY THE
NATIONAL FEDERATION OF WOMEN'S INSTITUTES: ESTABLISHED IN CONJUNCTION
WITH THE WOMEN'S BRANCH BOARD OF AGRICULTURE AND FISHERIES.

VOL. I.—No. 1.	MARCH, 1919.	PRICE 2d.

Chairman—THE LADY DENMAN.   *Vice-Chairman*—MISS GRACE HADOW.
Hon. Treasurer—MISS ALICE WILLIAMS.   *General Secretary* –MRS. KENYON.

All Communications should be addressed to THE EDITOR, "HOME AND COUNTRY," *National Federation of Women's Institutes*, 72, *Victoria Street, Westminster, S.W.*1.

PHOTO TAKEN AT W.I. EXHIBITION AT CAXTON HALL, OCTOBER, 1918.

FROM LEFT TO RIGHT
MRS. GODMAN, H.M. THE QUEEN, PRINCESS MARY, MISS ALICE WILLIAMS, MRS. ALFRED WATT.

Home and Country – *Cover of First Issue, March 1919.*

1918. In the picture is HM the Queen, Princess Mary, Miss Alice Williams and Mrs. Alfred Watt. So this first exchange of ideas which Lady Denman felt would be very helpful 'promised that village would be united to village and county to county in a way which had never been possible before. That this exchange of ideas should lead to Institute members being bound every year into a closer comradeship is the sincere wish of G.Denman, Chairman National Federation'. The 'G' stands for Gertrude although she was known as Trudie, but probably only called this by her closest friends.

The subscription in 1919 was still 2s. and where there was a Federation members were asked to send 2d. for each member to the county. Those not having a County Federation were asked to send it direct to National. *Home & Country* itself cost 2d. per copy, and this first issue included notes on the work of Women's Institutes in some of the counties, the start of a WI at Sandringham at which Mrs. Alfred Watt spoke and which the Queen and Princess Mary attended, and a For Sale column as well as Competitions and Advertisements.

As you can imagine, at the end of the First World War there was a great deal of patriotism and much singing of songs by various organisations as well as waving of banners typified by the British Legion branches. Lady Denman felt the WI needed a patriotic song to sing at the beginning of all meetings and so a competition was launched to find a good but unknown poetess to write the words for the special arrangement of *Jerusalem* which had been given at the Annual General Meeting by Sir Walford Davies and had been written by Sir Hubert Parry. Miss Hadow took the view that poetry written for a special purpose was unlikely to be good and so when a verse was received which started 'We are a band of earnest women' Lady Denman had to agree with her and the idea was abandoned. Instead National Executive decided to go with the words of *Jerusalem* –

        And did those feet in ancient times
           Walk upon England's mountains green?
        And was the Holy Lamb of God
           On England's pleasant pastures seen?
        And did the countenance divine
           Shine forth upon our clouded hills?
        And was Jerusalem builded here
           Amongst those dark, satanic mills?

> Bring me my bow of burning gold!
>   Bring me my arrows of desire!
> Bring me my spear! Oh clouds, unfold!
>   Bring me my chariot of fire!
> I will not cease from mental fight,
>   Nor shall my sword sleep in my hand,
> Till we have built Jerusalem
>   In England's green and pleasant land.

Apparently when Blake had written Jerusalem he had thought of it not as a heavenly city but rather a state of mind which was attained by practising the virtues of love and the healing power of constructive imagination. He believed to achieve this state of mind people would have to live in harmony with each other, practising mutual tolerance and working for each other's good, and although we may each of us put our own interpretation on all his words his belief was that only by using one's knowledge and imagination and by working together in love can a solution of the world's problems be found. Jerusalem was therefore adopted by the WI and in the early days it was sung at the beginning of all meetings with God Save the King being sung before it or, more usually, at the end of meetings.

Following the first Consultative Council meeting in Leicester two more were held in Bristol and York. The Council was composed of a representative from each County Federation and was to meet thrice a year, not necessarily in London, to confer with the National Executive. So what has been achieved by 1920 – National has been established with its first AGM being held in 1917, the first VCOs were appointed in 1918; Home & Country was launched in 1919 together with Consultative Councils and in 1920 the Guild of learners leading to Handicraft Guilds had been started. Counties, too, were gradually becoming affiliated to the National Federation so that we begin to see a National organisation developing. Sussex was the first county in 1917 with more joining the ranks by 1919 of which Northamptonshire was one. In those early days we were The Northamptonshire and Soke of Peterborough Federation of Women's Institutes.

Chapter 3
CONSOLIDATION
1921–1927

It seems appropriate at the start of this new chapter to list the 10 successful candidates from the full list of 29 standing for this 1920 ballot for Executive so that we can learn something about these early members who were instrumental in getting the WI off the ground in Northamptonshire. Here they are in alphabetical order: Mrs. E.M. Barker (Earls Barton), Miss Mary Bouverie (Hardingstone), Miss Beatrice Cartwright (Brackley), Mrs. Dodson (Wootton), Mrs. C.B. Fisher (Clipston), Mrs. Gibson (Hardingstone), Mrs. Lloyd (Brigstock), Lady Horne (East Haddon), Lady Beatrice Stanley (Sibbertoft) and Mrs. J. Walker (Boughton). This ballot took place at the first Annual Council Meeting in December with the WI delegates voting for their Executive either before the meeting or during their lunch hour. They also voted for their President and on this occasion Lady Knightley (Badby) was elected.

The first meeting of Executive took place in January 1921. Can you imagine the picture? Ten ladies sitting in a semi-circle in a small office in Wellington Street, Northampton, papers on their knees – probably wearing their hats. The room had been rented at £60 per annum from the Gas Board. At this first meeting Miss Bouverie presided over the ballot for Chairman and Mrs. Lloyd was elected. She did however resign later in the year, in August, and it was decided that Mrs. Barker should act as Chairman for the remainder of the year. At the January 1922 meeting Miss Bouverie was elected Chairman and continued in this capacity until 1939.

The first event of 1921 took place in April and it was an Exhibition, Show and Sale of WI work which was held in the Town Hall in Northampton, admission 1s., after 5 pm 6d. WI members were only charged 3d. This was opened at 2 pm by Lady Isabel Margesson (Worcestershire) a member of the National Executive, and the prizes were presented by Lady Knightley.

Much credit was given to Miss Dodson of Wootton Rectory who had been the secretary of the Exhibition. The report in the *Northamptonshire Daily Chronicle* stated that 'nothing could have been more successful and illuminating than the hundreds of entries in the various classes which emphasised the ever widening sphere of women's work and completely shattered the prevalent cynical opinion that the modern members of the weaker sex have lost that charming knowledge and skill for providing homely and old-fashioned comforts – although this probably applies more to the town than to the country folk'. The Exhibition showed the really good work done by the Federation which at that time had only 41 WIs, stating it had worked 'assiduously for the promotion of social life in the villages, combined with the desire to make the daily round for the women living there of a more attractive and interesting nature. That the object had been eminently successful and satisfactory was plainly evidenced and the country owes a deep debt of gratitude to the energetic workers who have devoted their time to the cause.'

Women showed what they could do from growing carrots and making butter to knitting silk jumpers and home curing rabbit and mole skins. The section devoted to articles manufactured from waste products was of absorbing interest. 'Who would have thought it possible to knit a pair of fleecy white mittens on a spindle from wool gathered on the hedgerows? Very serviceable door mats were made from fragments of binding twine. A neat and elegant woollen dress was the outcome of legs from socks which had become too old for re-footing and odd scraps of leather had grown into a handsome fireside cushion.' Patchwork was prominent as was glove making. The special Challenge Urn awarded to the WI gaining most prizes went to Hardingstone WI.

No account is given at the next Executive of the amount taken at this Exhibition, but it was decided that in future all bills were to be presented to the committee for approval and signed at the meeting. Proper accounts were to be drawn up so that they could be presented to future Council Meetings. Numbers of letters received and sent out were also to be recorded. The balance in hand was shown as £185 with the need for a grant from National getting less each year.

The next event was a 'Women's Rally' held on 23rd June 1921 at Delapre Abbey. On that Tuesday morning 'charabancs and motors full of ladies started from all parts of the county to converge upon Delapre Park. The occasion was a grand rally to enable the members to meet and join in an outing on the same day. Parties set out as early as 8 o'clock, and every institute in the county, except for two, was represented. Altogether members attended from 43 institutes. Old as well as young ladies were present, and many enthusiasts, in addition to bringing provisions, brought their babies.'

There had been some confusion over the provision of tea and eventually Miss Bouverie and her WI, Hardingstone, stepped into the breach and provided tea at the low cost of 1s. per head In addition to permitting the Rally to be in Delapre Park, Miss Bouverie made most of the arrangements for the reception of visitors, the chief of whom was Lady Denman, the National Chairman. As it was impossible to seat all 1,200 visitors at once, ladies who could not find chairs sat on the lawn to hear Lady Denman's address, and a few it is reported even sat on the gravelled path so that they could hear properly. Lady Denman said she had always thought of Northamptonshire as the county in which she had enjoyed some of the best hunting of her life, but in future she would regard it as the county which produced the best women's institutes! She talked about the work of the National Federation telling members that their expenditure was £10,000 annually. The institutes provided £2,000 of this by way of affiliation fees and donations, with the shortfall being covered by a grant of £8,000 from the government. Lady Denman appealed to everyone to realise the value of the work done by the National and County Federations and to give them their wholehearted support. At this time there were 2,100 members nationally. The Rally seems to have been a successful event, finishing with tea, and children folk dancing and singing.

The first idea of a Music Festival was mooted this year, the members having had an inspiring talk from Lady Lavinia White at a Council meeting. She explained the objects and scope of the Music Competition Festival held in Northampton and told members that a class was to be set apart for Women's Clubs. Incidentally this was won at the next Festival by Clipston. WI holidays took on a new meaning for 1921. They were invariably just summer outings to places like Bedford, Peterborough, Leicester, Lilford, Stratford upon Avon, Oxford and Burghley, nearly all of them being preceded by a lecture on the place to be visited. A train trip to Wembley was organised for the British Empire Exhibition, 300 to be guaranteed. Lunch would be organised at Lyons – what memories that name evokes, with waitresses all in black and their little white aprons and caps.

The next Council meeting was held in the Exchange Assembly Rooms in 1922. 37 delegates attended the morning session with 132 members attending in the afternoon. This was when mention was made of the Books and Library Schemes which had been set up in some Federations before the days of Public and Travelling Libraries. Miss Hadow, National Vice-Chairman had been the driving force behind them being started in Oxfordshire. It was after hearing Miss Deneke of

"FOR HOME AND COUNTRY."

KING'S SUTTON AND CHARLTON
Women's Institute
1922

President : MRS. METCALFE.
Vice-Presidents : LADY BROWN and MISS DAGLEY.
Treasurer : MISS HARMAN.   Secretary : MISS HARPER.

COMMITTEE :

MRS. CADD	MRS. HERMON	MRS. WHITEHEAD
MRS. FISHER	MRS. SPOKES	MISS WILLIAMS
MISS FALCONER	MRS. STANTON	
MRS. HEATH	MISS WARD	

Annual Membership Fee is 2/-

Anyone wishing to join must be proposed by a member of the Committee.

The Meetings are held on the first Tuesday of the month, unless otherwise arranged.

A Suggestion Box is kept at the Post Office and is available at all meetings. Members are asked to use it freely.

A Stall will be in readiness for any articles a member may wish to sell. One Penny in the shilling to be deducted from the sales for Institute expenses.

The Library is open at the Reading Room from 4.30 to 5.30 on Wednesdays. Annual Subscription 1/-

Classes will be held on Rush-work, Slippers, Blouses, etc. Particulars from Miss Williams.

Subscriptions for the Clothing Club are taken by Miss Harman on Mondays at the Schools; and at Mrs. Tilbury's house when Miss Harman is away.

"*HOME & COUNTRY*" Monthly Journal 2/4½ yearly.

Certificates given for Competitions, and Prizes of value at the end of the year.

PROGRAMME

February 20th. *"Actions speak louder than words."*
Talk on "Local Government." MISS BEATRICE CARTWRIGHT.
Demonstration : "Housewifery." MISS D. BRAITHWAITE.
Competition : Darning.
Games. Refreshments. Market Stall.

March 7th. *"Know Everything about Something, and Something about Everything."*
Demonstration : "Household Jobbery."
Competition : Orange Marmalade.
Refreshments. Market Stall. Country Dancing and Music.

April 25th. *"Progress ever, stand still never."*
Demonstration : "Upholstery."
Competition : "Best cooked dinner for a working man for 1/6."
Refreshments. Adderbury Friends. Market Stall.

May 9th. *"A little Help is worth much Pity."*
Talk on "How to get rich quickly." MISS RAVENSHAW. (London)
Competition : Crocheted Hat or Cap.
Refreshments. Mrs. Jarley's Waxworks. Market Stall.

June 20th. *"Who will remember that skies are grey, If he carries a happy heart all day?"*
Garden Meeting. Country Dances. Guessing Competitions.
American Stall for Clothing Club Bonus. Tea.
Competition : "Something New from Something Old."

July 4th. *"'Tis England's need that bids her Women no more be dull."*
Garden Meeting. Poultry Show and Sports.
Competition : Child,s Apron or Pinafore for 1/-
Tea. Market Stall.

August 1st. *"Keep in the sunlight, nothing beautiful grows in the darkness."*
Garden Meeting. Baby Show. Pastoral Play.
Competition : Jumper or Jersey.
Tea. Market Stall.

September 5th. *"If you've anything to give, that another joy might live—Give it."*
Lecture : "Herbs and their Use."
Competition : Blouse.
Tea. Market Stall. Amusement.

October 3rd. *"There is no study that is not capable of delighting us, after a little application."*
Lecture : "King's Sutton in the Olden Days."
Competition : Article made from ¼ lb of wool.
Old Fashioned Dances and Show of Old Things.
Market Stall. Refreshments.

November 7th. *"Wit without learning is like a tree without fruit."*
Lantern Lecture, Market Stall. Miscellaneous. Refreshments.
Competition : Pastry.

December 7th. *"Business first, Pleasure afterwards."*
ANNUAL MEETING.

This Programme is subject to alterations.

Oxfordshire speak on this subject that it was decided the matter should be referred to the new Executive Committee to discuss. The ballot for Executive which was undertaken annually resulted in the Hon. Mrs. Ferguson (Polebrook), Mrs. Gawthrop (Quinton & Courteenhall) and Mrs. Renton (Guilsborough) being added to the committee numbers. A resolution 'that the expenses of all delegates to Council meetings be pooled' was carried. This later caused problems in the office as it was quite unworkable owing to the expense of collecting fares from the WIs so the resolution was rescinded at another Council meeting and it was decided that all WIs should be responsible for their own delegates' expenses. A second resolution 'that a one-day school for Presidents, Vice-Presidents and Secretaries be held either separately or on the same day' was carried.

Mrs. Nugent Harris attended the meeting and presented certificates to 11 members whose work was accepted for the National exhibition at the Victoria & Albert Museum in May 1922. At the Annual Council Meeting at the end of the year Miss Simpson spoke of the advantage of the Group system and how it saved on expenses in transport when an 'expensive demonstrator is touring'. A VCO from Huntingdon followed Miss Simpson to explain that the objects in the minds of the Federation when starting the grouping system were threefold: 1} to economise on transport, 2} to save work at the County Headquarters, and 3} to give each group a VCO to 'mother' it. The VCO in charge would know her group thoroughly, its peculiarities and its difficulties. She would remind secretaries about important meetings, paying affiliation fees, etc. She would preside over Group Conferences which were very helpful as many Institute secretaries were unable to get to meetings in the County town. These Conferences were to be held quarterly and all VCOs should meet and report every month. At the end of the speeches it was proposed and carried 'that the grouping system be adopted for one year and then be readjusted if necessary'. Group conferences then were generally for committee members only and so were a great help in the running of WIs as the committees could get together and exchange ideas at these meetings, both with each other and with the VCOs. When some WIs asked for all members to be allowed to attend they were told this was impossible as the halls would not hold large numbers.

Following this resolution many WIs began voluntarily to work and to meet together, thus forming the Groups. The WIs chose which grouping they wished to have and one WI was known to have said that if they could not belong to a particular group they would move to another county! Groups over the years have been a great help providing stalls at events, staging area events and supporting the Federation wherever possible. However, they have never been part of the National Constitution, and where they do still exist they cannot hold funds and are accountable to the County Federation.

Remember that we are talking about our first Council and Executive meetings and Executive members were all feeling their way through their own county financial and administrative affairs, as well as taking on board National decisions. One of these decisions was to ask each Institute for a fixed sum each September bearing in mind their geographical position, activities and size and capacity for raising money. It was pointed out that the 'number of institutes is growing so fast that propaganda work costs far more now'. For propaganda I think we should read 'publicity' nowadays. Some counties appointed a Propaganda sub-committee but Northamptonshire felt this could well come under the remit of Executive or Organisation in that it seems to have involved promoting the organisation with a view to forming more WIs.

Another example of the Federation feeling its way is shown when a resolution was presented stating that if members do not attend 6 meetings during the year they should cease to be a member. Although this was discussed fully, it was eventually dismissed as it was felt this was a matter for each WI to settle for itself, being careful that no byelaw should limit membership. Mrs. Nugent Harris spoke on a model monthly meeting and a roll call was held on 'What is your WI doing for the young people of the village?'

Votes of Thanks were given to both the President and Chairmen at Council Meetings, in that there was a Proposer, and a Seconder, and this was then endorsed by everyone present with a show of hands.

The Library Books Scheme was gaining pace and it was reported that nearly 300 books had been bought or received from members and friends and that a grant of £16 had been made by the Rebecca Hussey Book Charity. It was now July and it was hoped the Library would be working by October. Books would be changed every 3 months and WIs would be charged 30 shillings for 20 books. Members would then borrow books from their WI for a small fee. Shelves had been fitted at the Federation Office. They were plain deal which could be stained if thought necessary. Arrangements had been made for one Executive member to be in attendance one day a week to receive boxes – carriage paid by the county.

Here we are again in December with the Annual Council Meeting being held only days away from Christmas. Members must have been much more organised then as 46 WIs were represented and delegates were able to get away from home in spite of Christmas coming up in the next ten days.

Resolutions adopted were (1) That the objects of Group meetings be clearly stated (2) That WIs would welcome visits from a member of the Executive Committee twice yearly. An amendment was moved that members of the Executive Committee be *invited* to visit WIs. which was carried, and (3) That the June Council meeting should be a movable one and be held in different towns.

The idea of a Rest and Change Scheme was discussed. This offered hospitality to members anywhere in the country who wished to have a rest in another area, in other words to have a short holiday to recuperate following illness, at no expense. All WIs would be circulated asking for offers of accommodation if this idea was approved. Members agreed this Scheme should be adopted as well as the starting of a Guild of Learners of Home Crafts which National had already started. In looking at what had been achieved by 1923, therefore, we have a County Federation, an elected Executive, a Group system, Library and Rest Schemes being set up and the following sub-committees appointed:

ORGANISATION, FINANCE, HANDICRAFTS, LIBRARIES, and **EXHIBITIONS.**

To give an overall picture of what these sub-committees were doing, here is a brief outline of their work in this particular year. All committees had at least three members of Executive serving on them and so the meetings were held on a Saturday, with Executive at 1.45 and the other meetings either earlier at 11.30 or following Executive in the afternoon. The expenses of committee members were paid.

ORGANISATION was to be responsible for the care of new WIs for the first three months after formation, membership consisting of 8 VCOs with Group Conveners being invited twice a year. Miss Bouverie was Chairman, with Mrs. Gibson (Hardingstone) Hon. Secretary.

Early in April Miss Simpson had organised a school for Secretaries and Treasurers with 46 members attending from 31 WIs. This was followed by a School for Presidents and Vice- Presidents, this time with an attendance of 56 from 41 WIs.

When the time for VCO reappointments came up at the end of the year, it was agreed at Executive that only 7 should be reappointed. A ballot took place and there was a tie for the 7th place. This was resolved by asking the members who had not attended that particular Executive meeting to record their votes for the 7th place and thus decide who should be retained and who dropped. National agreed to pay £1 to Counties for each VCO they recommended for reappointment.

There were 66 WIs by the end of 1923.

FINANCE was responsible for ensuring the Federation funds were adequate, and as the situation fluctuated such a great deal it was decided to explain the position to WIs telling them how dependent the Federation was on money raising events to help meet expenses. One of the suggestions made to WIs was that they might like to borrow £1 for trading purposes to see what profit they could made which would then be sent to the county.

National had requested a donation for Miss Inez Ferguson, General Secretary on the occasion of her wedding – 10/6d. was sent.

It had been decided at Executive that a Federation Secretary should be appointed at a salary of £102 per annum, and Mrs. Barker agreed to take this position. Right from the very beginning she had, in fact, being doing a great deal of work from her home in Moulton. It soon became obvious, even with the appointment of a secretary, that there was still too much office work to do so an Hon. Treasurer was appointed as well as a Home & Country Correspondent, both of which offices still exist to-day.

HANDICRAFTS were to be responsible for furthering interest in handicrafts in the institutes through the Handicraft Guild, Mrs. Renton (Guilsborough) to be Chairman.

A Loan Collection was to be started with WIs being asked to send in suitable items to be put together in a display which could be hired out to WIs. This was later abandoned as it was felt fashions changed too quickly.

Handicraft classes continued in glove making, fine embroidery and basketry. These classes were usually followed by Shopping Days organised so that members could send in items for sale and were held in November at Delapre Abbey. It was agreed at first to hold Dramatic competitions and provide teas on these Days, but later it was decided to keep Drama separate and hold Shakespearean competitions in the Town Hall in December. A prize of two guineas had been offered by Mr. Travis of the Northampton Art School for the best designed costume produced under his supervision. Executive were happy to accept this if they could choose the winner.

LIBRARIES to be responsible for setting up and running a county scheme, Chairman Mrs. Dodson (Wootton). A Librarian was eventually appointed and new books needed to be bought quite frequently as the Scheme proved extremely popular. A comprehensive typed catalogue was produced. The County Council eventually decided to adopt the Carnegie Rural Libraries scheme and hoped WIs would help by providing voluntary librarians to take charge in all villages where there was a WI. The Federation agreed to help wherever possible.

EXHIBITION to be responsible for stalls, etc. at Rallies and Shows – Rushton Hall Rally to be held in April 1923 and the Kettering Show Whit Monday 1923. Mrs. Wentworth Watson was appointed Chairman of this committee and at that time she was President of Stoke Albany WI, there not being a WI at Rockingham until later when she became President of both WIs with the approval of Executive.

To give you a flavour of the County Fete/Rally held at Rushton Hall it was reported at the time that between five and six thousand residents from a very wide area attended this gathering having wended their way by road or rail. The fete was opened by the Marchioness of Northampton and in her introduction of her Lady Knightley said the ideal of the WI to make England a brighter and happier place was brought to the front during the war when everybody wanted to do what they could for the men who fought for them. Mrs and Miss Breitmeyer were thanked for having allowed the use of their beautiful grounds. (Rushton Hall is now a well-known hotel.)

A tennis tournament was held and two pageants entitled 'Come lassies and lads' were performed in the quadrangle. This was followed by country dancing by children attired in various coloured dresses of the period. Sir Roger de Coverley was one of the dances and was 'exceptionally picturesque'. Attractions galore drew the attention of the numerous visitors on every hand. These included Digging for Hidden Treasure, Bowling for Ducks, Lucky Balloons, Darts, Hoop'la, Skittling for Pigs, Candle Lighting Board and a Spinning Lizzie. Ice Cream, Lemonade and Fruit Salad were all available and had been kindly donated.

Up-to-date music was provided by the Kettering Town Band. There is no record of the takings at the Rally but the Kettering Show resulted in a profit of £178.17.1d from the various side shows and stallholders.

Burleigh House was to be the venue for the next Rally to be held on Whit Monday 1924 and was to be a joint venture with the Nursing Association with Mrs. Renton as Chairman. To finish with **Executive's** achievements this year, it was decided that a diary should be made available for sale and 1,000 were purchased for £3.19s.

The National Federation were taking a tent at the Royal Show, and Northamptonshire, in line with all other surrounding Federations, would guarantee £5 for expenses, as well as stewards for one afternoon. 29 articles were sent for sale after having been carefully selected by the committee.

A letter and circular from the Ministry of Health re cancer was to be sent to all WIs. Miss Bouverie reported from National that they thought the Northamptonshire grouping system was the best in use at present – no elections for conveners, just recommendations from Organisation with a VCO in charge; also that members of the Executive were more active than other counties and did much more visiting. It was at this time that Miss Bouverie reported she had been elected Chairman of the Finance Committee of the National Federation, and was thus the National Federation Treasurer.

The local Press had been contacted asking for a WI column but so far 'not inclined to help'. Letters received were generally around 200 with more than 300 being sent out. Mrs. Luddington VCO of Milton Malsor was co-opted to the committee.

These early days were obviously very busy and very productive, and moving on to 1924 we now have news of another sub-committee, **HISTORY, MUSIC & DRAMA**. This was set up to deal with the great interest there was in Drama in the WIs, to oversee the Castle Ashby Rally to be held in 1925, and to liaise with Mrs. Fisher on her suggestion for a village history to be compiled in each area.

Mrs. Fisher reported on the History scheme at the next Half-Yearly Council held at Brackley Town Hall in June 1924 and told members that this was being worked on by Miss Joan Wake of Courteenhall. Mrs Fisher had been responsible for the Book of Clipstone, a history of her own village, and Miss Wake's book was to be a guide to any institute in the county desiring to undertake a similar venture. Miss Wake stated 'history is no longer regarded as being merely the record of celebrities and of great events. These have their place, but the history of England is incomplete without an account of the ordinary man and woman in their doings in all walk and conditions of life. Every village is teeming with interest and historical information, only waiting to be revealed by well-directed enthusiasm. It cannot be emphasised too often that fascinating as is the task of digging out history from written records and the memories of the old, the most valuable part of the work that is likely to be done by the local historian is the record which he keeps of that which he has witnessed with his own eyes.'

This was obviously to be a competition between WIs to see which could write the best Village History. Miss Wake offered prizes of one guinea and 10/6d for essays written by members living in houses of not more than 6s. rental or £5 rateable value.

A letter had been received from a speaker stating she had been 'lodged very roughly and unfortunately in a small and very cold room in a labourer's cottage. The landlady has done her best but never have I had such quarters in 25 years travel up and down the country speaking for the suffrage and many other causes. I shall think twice before accepting another engagement for the WI.'

The 1925 Half-Yearly Council meeting was to be held at Thrapston when Mrs. Inez Jenkins (nee Ferguson) would speak on the work of National and County Federations and Miss Simpson would have a roll call on 'What does your Institute appreciate most in the work of the Federation?' Mrs. Jenkins was National Secretary from 1919-1929, marrying in 1923. When World War II started she was appointed Chief Administrative Officer of the Women's Land Army working alongside Lady Denman again. She held this position until 1949 when she was awarded the CBE for her war work. In 1953 she wrote 'The History of the WI Movement in England and Wales'.

First mention is made here of Miss Agnes Stops (Duston) whose name was being sent forward for an advanced VCO School at Chester, which she attended under the tuition of Lady Denman.

One of the first duties of the 1925 Executive was to update the office. Firstly, a new typewriter was bought for £12, a committee table was needed (fortunately one was offered by a member of the committee), the room needed to be painted and it was decided this should be yellow. A duplicator was to be bought as it had been agreed to consider a duplicated Federation Newsletter which could be sent to all members. The secretary's salary was to be increased by £25 per annum.

£85 had been sent to National being £1 per WI which was a considerable sum bearing in mind the subscription was still set at 2s. per member – the figure which had been set originally by National, being one-tenth of the agricultural wage.

Because of an outbreak of smallpox at Kettering, the half-yearly

Council meeting was to be re-arranged and held at the YWCA Rooms in Northampton and the speaker was Mr. Morris from Farthinghoe whose subject was Drama.

At last, December dates for events were being queried, members asking if these could not be held earlier in the year.

The Shopping Days this year had become a Shopping Week – still in November – and was to be held in the Gas Board demonstration hall, 2d. in the £1 from all sales to be retained by the county.

The *Reminder*, a Kettering newspaper which cost 2d. per month offered to be a WI paper. After consulting members, it was agreed this should happen.

One of the first events to be recorded in the *Reminder* was the Fete and Rally held at Castle Ashby in July which was written by 'Our Special Correspondent' This comprehensive article tells us that the Marchioness of Exeter (wife of the Lord Lieutenant of the County) opened the Fete from the entrance to the courtyard and as she came through the door, charmingly dressed in a dress of green printed crepe de chine and a brown hat, the WI massed choir of over a thousand voices broke into Parry's beautiful hymn Jerusalem. The accompanist was Mrs. Walter of Islip. Lady Knightley as President welcomed Lady Exeter and then spoke of the Rest and Change Scheme as well as the proposed scheme of historical research which would probably result in the compilation of a history and present-day record of village life. In declaring the fete open, Lady Exeter said all honour was due to those who organised the work of the WI which did so much to brighten the lives and widen the outlook of the women who lived in country districts. 'Any organisation of this kind which is non-sectarian and non-party political must prove a valuable force for the common good and for strengthening and fostering friendly feeling in all.'

The Fete had been organised by all sub-committees with the addition of ad hocs for Grounds, Entertainment and Refreshments.

The Handicraft Tent was a great source of interest and demonstrations could be seen in the art of basket work, sweet making, raffia and embroidery. Attractions were provided in every corner of the grounds, a tennis tournament attracted 20 couples, concerts were given at intervals and teams from Pitsford and Market Harborough gave exhibitions of folk dancing.

Stalls had been provided by many WIs and an Executive member was in charge of each group – Lady Spencer home produce, the Hon. Mrs. Ferguson mineral waters, Miss Bouverie ladder golf, Miss Cartwright handkerchiefs, Lady Lilford balloon football, Lady Wake

This is the first photograph of our early Federation Officers that has come to light. It was taken immediately after the opening ceremony of the Fete and Rally at Castle Ashby on Thursday, 9 July 1925. From left to right: Miss Beatrice Cartwright, J.P., C.C., Mrs. Gawthropp, **Mrs. Barker** *(County Secretary), Mrs. Renton,* **Lady Knightley** *(County Federation President), Hon. Mrs. Ferguson, The Marchioness of Northampton (Hostess), The Marchioness of Exeter (Opener), Lady Horne,* **Miss Bouverie***, J.P. (Chairman of the County Executive), Mrs. C.B. Fisher, and Countess Spencer.*

croquet bowling, Mrs. Renton flowers, Miss Lloyd surprise packets, Lady Manningham Buller hidden treasure. The chairman of the organising committee was Mrs. Renton, with Mrs. Barker as her secretary and they were thanked by the Federation Chairman Miss Bouverie. It seems to have been a very colourful event, much enjoyed by all who attended. The book to be published by Miss Joan Wake had been completed and 500 copies were ordered at a cost of £18. Before the end of the year another 1,500 were ordered, National having requested 500 on sale/return. Copies were in all booksellers and libraries.

In December 1925 the first Shakespearean Drama Competition was held which was judged by Sir Frank Benson, apparently a cousin of Lady Wake. It was reported at the time 'that it was perhaps as well that few people outside the WI knew he would be attending otherwise it is doubtful whether the Town Hall would have held all those anxious to meet the famous actor off the stage. His presence, no doubt, acted as a spur to the competitors, who put their very best into their work drawing from their judge much sincere and gratifying praise. His speech should do much to stir up even greater enthusiasm in the theatrical side of WI activities.'

SHARED MEMORIES

The Marchioness of Exeter opening the Fete.

Lady Horne and helpers.

Lady Knightley, of Fawsley.

Lady Spencer in charge of home produce stall.

Drama Competitions continued over the next three years and in 1926 the headlines were 'Good Acting, Charming Dress, but Oh those Beards!' All the judges for these competitions were well known and from the British Drama League. This year's competition had two classes, one for comedy and one for tragedy. Modern plays were omitted, but Shakespeare was still the playwright featured. The judge, a Mr. Cyril Wood, said 'I knew it was going to be an unusual experience as my work is confined almost entirely to the professional theatre and professional actors. Frankly, he had thought it was going to be a terribly dull day. Instead of that, however, it had 'been a most interesting experience, and in many ways rather educational from my point of view.'

The entries had increased from 12 to 18, and Shakespeare had given way to more modern plays such as *The Old Streak* by Roland Pertwee, *The Princess and the Woodcutter* by A.A.Milne and *Honest Folk* by F. Austin Hyde. Points were given by the judge for choice of scene, number of actors and the equal dividing of work, clearness of speech, grouping, interpretation of character and ingenuity in dress. Commenting upon the performance of Brackley WI, the judge said 'it was exceedingly good, more especially because of the work of the lady who took the part of the gardener – hers was a fine piece of character acting.' The sub-committee Chairman for all these Dramatic Competitions was Mrs. Wentworth Watson, and Lady Henley of Watford featured not only on the committee but was one of the star performers – she appears to have had a dramatic background as she had been an actress. No restrictions then on who was eligible to enter competitions or festivals, the concept being to show the best the WI had to offer. Finally in 1925 the Annual Council meeting was held but no speaker had been booked so Miss Simpson led a discussion on 'What have our WIs done to help others during the year?' Following this meeting two more members were co-opted to the 1926 Executive, Mrs. Atterbury of West Haddon and Miss Clare of Towcester; both were also to serve on the Handicrafts sub-committee.

1926 saw the demise of the LIBRARY sub-committee as the WI Library scheme had ceased to exist the County Council having taken over this role. Mrs. Gawthropp became the Federation representative on their committee which kept the WI in touch with the current position. This could be regarded as a great WI achievement, a simple books and lending library system in rural areas leading to such libraries being provided by the County Council. 1926 also saw the start of another sub-committee, **AGRICULTURE & HORTICULTURE**.

The organisation has always had agricultural ties as it was members of the Agricultural Organisation Society who were instrumental in the early days in giving support to the WI. So when the suggestion of Produce Shows and attendance at County Agricultural Shows became a possibility it was inevitable that such a committee would be appointed. The Federation had been asked by National to support a School for training agricultural students and to give hospitality to the 12 students involved. This eventually took place with the help of Moulton Farm Institute, and National were extremely pleased with the whole event. It seems appropriate here to say that the WI has always had very close links with Moulton.

The Moulton Farm Institute was established in 1920 with the purchase of Home Farm and two detached houses and their grounds and four cottages for farm staff. The first principal was Mr. W.A. Stewart MA, BSc as from 1st January and the first students were received on 16th October 1921. There were 15 men, 11 of whom were resident, and the course lasted two terms. During the year the growing requirements for poultry keeping and dairying showed a need for a Dairy Poultry Instructress and on 29th July 1922 Miss J.W. Strang, NDD, at that time in charge of the Royal Dairy at Balmoral, was appointed to the post and took up her appointment on 10th October of that year.

Miss Strang and Mr. Lawrence from the College both became members of the Agriculture & Horticulture sub-committee and through the years helped to develop the WI interest in providing and growing good food, and were invaluable in setting up classes for WI members in all these aspects.

For the Council meeting at Northampton in December 1926 Mr. Gotch of Kettering spoke on the History of the County of Northampton.

The financial statement at the end of the year showed current account at £91.8.6d. and £114 in the deposit/fete account.

Space was again provided for the WI at the County Agricultural Show at Delapre in May for a Show and Sale of Handicrafts, and members of the Executive gave a cup for the Northampton Musical Festival for choirs from villages over 500 people, Lady Thorne already having presented a cup for those under 500 population.

The *Women's Institute First Song Book* was published about this time and copies were available from National at 2d. each, increasing to 3d. by 1927. Songs featured included 'Dashing away with the Smoothing Iron', 'The Jolly Plough Boy', 'Drink to me Only', The Bluebells of

Scotland' and a note at the beginning of the book when talking about the great usefulness of accustoming members to singing without a piano goes on to state 'Though possibly there may be some hesitation at first, if every singer can have the music before them, gradually the connection between the sounds and the notes is acquired, and with some slight explanation and help the singing voice becomes a real factor in enjoyment'.

A special sub-committee was set up to manage the 1927 Fete & Rally. This was to take place at Althorp, with Lady Denman as the special guest. It was suggested a Produce Show should form part of the day, which is in fact what happened, but later it was reported that combining with a Fete & Rally had not been entirely successful and future Produce Shows should be organised separately.

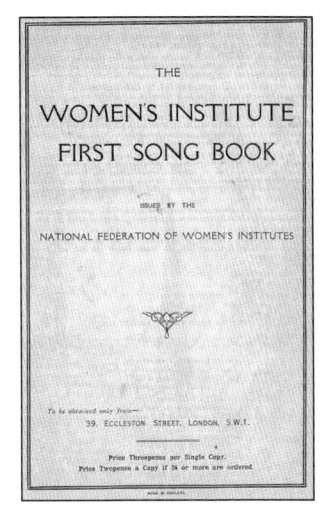

In the office an Assistant Secretary was engaged at £40 per annum for 3 days a week and the holiday period for staff was fixed for July/August. The idea of a county badge was discussed and eventually 150 were ordered in the form of a bar with the wording 'Northamptonshire' printed across them. These were obtained from Messrs. Fattorini, a firm which is still supplying WI badges to this day.

The year ended with the usual Annual Council Meeting in December at which Mrs. Gervase Huxley, a member of the National Executive spoke on the Hampshire Scheme for the Alteration of the Constitution of the NFWI. Mrs. Huxley started her talk in her capacity as National Treasurer by appreciating the fact that Northamptonshire and five other counties were the only ones who had paid the full quota asked for during the last four years. Going on to explain the Hampshire Scheme Mrs. Huxley said the general policy of the National Federation would be decided by the Annual General Meeting as before. A National Council would be selected which would elect an Executive Committee to carry out the policy laid down by the Annual Meeting.

The National Council would consist of (a) one representative from each County Federation elected by the Institutes of that county by postal ballot, the elected members to become ex officio a member of the County Federation Executive Committee (b) members of the National

Federation Executive Committee, (c) representative members appointed by Government departments (d) the National Council and the Executive Committee would have one and the same Chairman. The Council would meet quarterly to receive from Executive a report of its work for the past quarter, The Council would consider and confirm, amend or reject, the recommendations received from Executive and would deal with all the communications addressed direct to the National Council.

The new Executive would consist of 12 to 15 members elected annually by the National Council on the nominations of members of the National Council. The Executive Committee would have the same powers of co-option as heretofore, and candidates for the Committee need not necessarily be themselves members of the National Council. The functions of the Executive Committee would remain as at present except that it would be required to report quarterly to the National Council. The Executive Committee would also have the power to appoint sub- committees as at present, but it would be necessary that a fixed proportion of the members should be members of the National Council Furthermore the National Council would replace the present Consultative Council.

It must be remembered that at this time there were many new ideas being put forward and this one defining who Hampshire thought should be the administrative body of the WI was just one of them. It was eventually defeated at a National Annual General Meeting probably because members were not directly involved with the election of the National Executive members.. The Northamptonshire Annual meeting at which Mrs. Huxley spoke was held in the Council Chambers at County Hall because the WI had outgrown its usual venue of the YWCA Hall, and there were five resolutions on the agenda.

The number of WIs in Northamptonshire at 1st January 1927 was 95, with 3,749 nationally. The full distribution of these was shown on the cover of *Home & Country* for this issue.

Chapter 4
BRANCHING OUT
1928–1935

1928 was a very auspicious year for many reasons – it was the year of the Equal Franchise Act by which women over 21 had the right to vote, Mickey Mouse first appeared on screen, the Townswomen's Guilds were started, Alexander Fleming invented penicillin, Neville Chamberlain addressed the 13th AGM of the National Federation, but most importantly from my point of view it was the year I was born! I know this history is not about me, but it is very difficult to write objectively all the time, so I hope you will forgive my occasional lapses into autobiography and in fact perhaps enjoy some of my memories. I know whenever I visited WIs they were fascinated by one's background, and so I always started off with a guessing game as to which year I was born quoting the more illustrious happenings.

Back to business, WI life carried on apace. Northamptonshire now had 98 WIs and the two new members of the 1928 Executive were Mrs. Brudenell (Deene) and Mrs. Steward (Brigstock). The Half Yearly Council meeting to be held at the YWCA was to have Miss Hadow speaking on Rural Community Councils and Mrs. Brudenell leading Community Singing.

The Fete & Rally in 1928 took the form of an Elizabethan Fayre at Fawsley Park the home of Sir Charles and Lady Knightley. It was reported that the Park 'seemed alive with the pageantry of the ages. Colour was weaved with colour; strange yet beautiful dresses moved across the grass smoothly and gracefully. Elizabethan maidens pirouetted here and danced the minuet there, while feminine charm plaited patterns on the maypole.' As was usual at all these events the WIs in the surrounding area were enlisted to help. There was 'much mirth, melody and merriment and the Fayre started with a pageant play *St Martin of Tours* (patron saint of Litchborough) and the theme of the play is naturally dignified and all the characters observed the spirit of the piece.'

Barely three months covered the whole period of rehearsal and time did not permit the amassing of what historical incidents might have been associated with the district. Mrs. Platt of Weedon who wrote and produced the play, therefore, had to visit each institute and write out a

Northamptonshire Federation of
Women's Institutes.
A GROUP PAGEANT.
**Old English Fair and
Historical Scenes**
WILL TAKE PLACE AT
DELAPRE ABBEY,
ON JULY 4th, 1928
(by kind permission of Miss Bouverie).
Performers from Hardingstone, Quinton
and Courteenhall, Wootton, Collingtree,
Milton, Hartwell, Ashton, Blisworth, and
Gayton.
ENTRANCE 1s. W.I. Members 6d. on
producing Badge or Membership Card.
Performers in costume Free.
First Performance 3 p.m. Reserved
Seats, first two rows, 2s. 6d.; rest, 1s.
Second Performance 7 p.m. Front seats,
1s.; rest 6d. TEA 1s.
SIDE SHOWS, BAND, DANCING.
Cars Parked, 2s. 6d. each.

Pageant notice, 1928.

scene for the guidance of members, at the same time keeping an eye on the cumulative effect when all such efforts merged into the final whole. That she accomplished this 'could easily be seen by the amusement that the Fayre afforded during the hour that it lasted'.

What with the unofficial – always there, the chastisements of the Crier, the antics of the Bear and the singing of 'Good Queen Bess' the scene was one of constant animation and perpetual amusement. Queen Bess finally headed the

An amusing episode – Dragon at Pageant

procession of performers off the grass and the spectators went away to look at the stalls which were scattered around the ground. The visitors also had the opportunity of talking to a fortune teller!

The Agriculture & Horticulture sub-committee was getting into its stride and it was decided to co-operate with Moulton Farm Institute for a 1929 Produce Show, and to help with the Tent at the County Agricultural Show at the end of May. As well as an Allotment competition it was agreed also to have a competition for Cottage Gardens. Butter making, fruit bottling and jam making classes were to be held at Moulton.

Earls Barton WI Choir had won the County Executive Committee cup and the Agnes Nicholls Shield at the Central Northants Musical Festival in March, securing ninety-one and ninety marks respectively for their rendering of the test pieces 'Blow, blow thou winter wind' and 'All through the Night'. The judge described their singing as magnificent and remarked that they had been wonderfully and most artistically trained. Their conductor was Mrs. Sidney Robinson.

A Drama School for Producers was held which 130 members attended. This was taken by Mr. Fay of the Abbey Theatre Dublin and he stated 'to get the spirit of a play over to the audience, the players must get into the characters themselves and be able if they were only doing part of a play to bring out each point in such a manner that the whole story, both before and after the scene takes place, could be realised'. Sketches of Stage Arrangements had been very helpful as had a Costume Parade. The Drama Competition at the Town Hall, which this year was based on verse speaking, competitors being given the choice of two poets, resulted in Guilsborough, Harlestone and Geddington gaining the first three places. Entries were not greatly increased and so new ideas were to be tried for future festivals, maybe by providing for mixed classes. It was at this time that Mrs. Adam Cross, Harlestone, presented two cups for Drama and they really are the most decorative and valuable cups in the possession of the Federation. At the time apparently they cost just £5 each.

As far as Organisation was concerned a ruling had been received from National that all VCOs must make at least 4 visits per year, and this is the first time we hear of a VCO not being reappointed through lack of work. In turning her down it was reported 'she had done very little VCO work and what she had done had not been successful'. You really had to justify your position and do your share of the work then. Nowadays we say please do as much as you can within the time available to you. A Competition for a Used Programme was initiated by this committee, and it was launched at the end of this year so that WIs could use their 1928 programmes.

Following the Used Programme competition it was decided to produce a skeleton headed WI Programme for the use of institute secretaries. One thousand were to be ordered and would cost £1.15.0d. Incidentally the winners of the competition were (1) Harlestone, (2) Castle Ashby and Brington (WIs under 100 members) and Brigstock, Brackley and Raunds (WIs over 100) A Craft Exhibition was held in October and over 57 WIs entered this event with a total of 660 entries, 450 of which received over 70% marks. This exhibition was opened by the Marchioness of Northampton and was held in the Town Hall, admission 1s., members 6d. Just to show the variety of classes included they are listed as needlework – handmade garment in crepe de chine or lawn – baskets, raffia work, gloves, leather articles, toys, weaving, slippers, men's shirts/pyjamas, embroidery – white/coloured in wool, silk, cross stitch – rugs and knitting. There was also a co-operative class which had to include a warm bedcover, box ottoman, baby's cot, anything in metal and photographs.

The financial statement to be presented at the Annual Council Meeting on 12 December showed a shortfall and an overdraft would have to be requested. This was less than previous months and so was deemed to be satisfactory. They really did live on the edge financially in the early years and Executive members frequently had to guarantee borrowings. The speaker at this meeting was from the NFU on Egg Marketing Reform – the Approved Scheme – with suggested packing cases and the discussion for members at the afternoon session was 'Absentee Members'! Community singing was conducted by Mrs. Sidney Robinson.

By 1929 we were in offices in the Raleigh Chambers, St. Giles Terrace, 60 Abington Street, still paying £60 per annum. Linoleum was bought for £7.7.11d. and a gas radiator hired for 12s. per annum. A duplicated monthly newsletter had been started 'incorporating any matters of importance arising from Executive or sub-committees which it is thought necessary for the Institutes to know'. It was in the form of a letter starting Dear Madam (to the WI Secretary) and ending Yours sincerely being signed by Mrs. Barker, the County Secretary. The comment was that they thought this would lead to a great saving! Certainly fewer letters would have to be written and office time might be used for other tasks. A new typewriter was bought for £12.

The Medical Officer of Health had visited Executive asking for help with his VD campaign. He wished to go to 15 towns and villages from mid-November to the end of December with a clinical van, lecturers and stalls displaying leaflets. It was agreed Groups be asked to arrange dates with the Medical Officer for afternoon visits. The National General Secretary, Mrs. Inez Jenkins, had resigned and a collection was to be organised – Northamptonshire sent £1.12.6d. towards this. Her successor was Dame Frances Farrer from Surrey, who was to remain in office until 1959.

Miss Agnes Stops, Duston, had been successful in her advanced VCO school in Chester. Her WI was unique in the county being the only one that met weekly from its time of formation in 1924 until 2004 when it sadly had to suspend. Miss Stops herself left the county shortly after taking the course in Chester, and moved to New Zealand as WI Organiser.

Again a Fete & Rally was held, this time at Lilford on 21 June, and the report read 'brilliant weather favoured the fete and rally and as it was arranged by the Northamptonshire Federation of Women's Institutes it was not a matter for surprise that the event was a gigantic success. Fully 2,000 visitors attended and hundreds of cars, charabancs and other vehicles conveyed them to the renowned gardens of the estate. The large attendance was a fitting testimony to the excellent work the movement is doing'.

Lady Knightley, in opening the proceedings after the singing of the National Anthem and the Institute's song 'Jerusalem' remarked that many of them might feel rather disheartened over their little gardens when they saw the beautiful grounds of Lilford, but she wished to remind them that a single plant would grow better in a cottage garden than in the grandest garden because it was the love of the woman who helped it to grow. England was the most beautiful country in the world, and it would be more so if they all resolved to make their gardens the best they possibly could. Lady Lilford, in declaring the fete open, said she was greatly impressed at the growing strength of the movement with 114 WIs now and a membership of between 6,000 and 7,000. It had been the means of finding marvellous talent and very often genius which would have never come to light if it had not been for the Institutes. Miss Bouverie then spoke and said she would like to point out the district's reputation for belladonna lilies, to which Lady Lilford replied 'I have seen nothing to equal them, but here, in the Hall grounds we cannot grow them!'

Prominent amongst the attractions was the Produce Show with classes for Cabbages, Stone Fruit, a bunch of wild flowers, (what would be said nowadays about this?), Honey, Brown hens' eggs, Fruit Cake,

White loaf, Home-made Wine, coloured or red. There was also a Handicraft Tent and excellent music was rendered by the Raunds Silver Band. A play *A Midsummer Nightmare* was arranged by Lady Henley. There were of course all the usual side shows supervised by local Institutes, but sadly the Tennis Tournament had to be abandoned through lack of entries!

Following the Rally the Handicraft sub-committee recommended that each Institute should be asked to appoint a Handicraft Secretary so that all handicraft matters could be sent to her in a quarterly letter. An exhibition had been held in the Town Hall at the end of May when the Half-Yearly Council meeting had been held in the morning. Lady Spencer had presented the prizes, and for the first time photography had been included and the subject was 'Any Rural Scene'. The awards this time were in the form of blue ribbons as National had said counties should not use gold stars as they might be confused with their awards.

As there were 22 entries for the Drama Competition the timing would have to be re-arranged and several institutes would have to perform on the Friday afternoon. Some felt the afternoon might prove difficult as most Institutes met in the afternoon but all appears to have gone off smoothly because all 22 entries appeared, 3 gaining 1st class, 8, 2nd class, 7, 3rd class and 5 nothing! Criticisms were to be sent to each WI with the next newsletter.

The Council Meeting at the end of the year had as its speaker Miss Fairfax from the International Council of Women, so here we are beginning to think of International affairs. A sister organisation, the Townswomen's Guilds, was set up in order to provide similar meetings to those of the WI but these, as the name implies, were to be in towns rather than rural areas. In fact, the WI was not permitted in those days to form Institutes where there was a population of more than 4,000.

The nomination paper for the 1929 Executive ballot had 39 names on it, and 12 members were elected. Once the ballot had taken place, additional Executive members were The Countess Spencer, Brington, Mrs. Hobson, Pattishall & Cold Higham, Lady Henley, Watford, and Mrs. Ripley, Wootton. Miss Corner, Creaton, was co-opted in April when she undertook the appointment of Consultative Council Representative.

The County Education Committee was to be written to making the following recommendations 1) that instruction in the preservation of fruit and vegetables and in food values should be included in the Summer Course at Moulton Farm Institute – no need at present for farm house management; 2) that the education of older children in elementary and central schools should have a rural bias and they wished particularly to stress the need for instruction in horticulture and the preservation of fruit and vegetables. The committee felt sure there was a great demand for practical demonstrations in jam-making, the preservation of fruit and vegetables and felt sure also there would be no difficulty in procuring 50 applications for the above. The Federation were receiving very pressing demands for cookery instruction and felt that there was a need for a part- time instructress in this subject and would point out that applications were having to be refused.

Mr. Holland, the Secretary to the County Education Committee attended the January Executive to explain the New Education Act. This decreed that the school age should be raised to 15 as from 1st April 1931 and all schools would have to be re-organised. Primary teaching would end at 11 and all education after that age would be secondary in type. Children would be put into smaller classes and their teachers would be all trained and certificated. All boys would be given instruction in handicrafts and girls would be taught domestic science including cookery, laundry and housewifery. This could not be done with schools as they were at that time and though the cost of carrying it out would be heavy it had to be done. Several villages would have to be linked together and all the children over 11 would be sent to one central school. This would involve an elaborate transport service, special arrangements for meals and for drying clothes.

Mr. Holland wished to have the scheme explained to WIs but promised to provide a memo containing all the necessary information. He wished parents to be shown that this was a great opportunity for their children and they must be prepared to make sacrifices. Executive agreed this matter should be explained through the Groups.

Another pressing matter at the time was the possible closure of the Domestic Economy School at Dallington in Northampton. Executive wrote to the County Council urging on behalf of the women of the county that the School be continued. They stated it was the only institution in the county providing exclusively for the technical training of women, as well as being the oldest of the schools established by the County Council. Housewifery, including cookery and laundry work, they stated was increasingly recognised as a skilled occupation, for which practical training was required and which offered many remunerative openings to women. The closure of the school would diminish the opportunities open to young women of the county for obtaining technical training, and the committee considered that these opportunities ought to be increased rather than diminished, especially as the age of compulsory school attendance was to be raised.

The Half-Yearly Council meeting was to have the Chief Constable, Mr. J. Williamson, to talk on 'Influence'. A discussion was to take place on which subject the WIs would like as a Golden Thread theme for 1931 – those suggested were Health and the Home, The Empire, Travel and Transport, and Our County. Our County was the subject eventually chosen. This, then, was to feature in all WI programmes as well as that of the county.

The County Banner* was actually started in 1922 but it was 1930 before it was finished, after which date it was carried to all County events. The materials to make it had cost 13s. and we still have it to-day hanging in WI House Also in 1930 there was a monthly typed newsletter being sent to 125 WIs.

The accounts for the Dramatic Competitions of the previous year had shown a deficit of at least £10 and Lady Henley agreed to be responsible for raising funds to offset this sum. A Garden Party was to be held at Watford Court, the home of Lady Henley, on 17 July and there were to be more side shows and stalls than previously to provide for County funds. The occasion was to be Fancy Dress and those not in costume would be charged 6d. admission. All Groups to be contacted for help. Advertising was to be taken up, one each in the Mercury, Herald, Chronicle and the Echo, so it would appear that these four newspapers were separate papers at that time.

A Drama School was to be held on Thursday, 17 March, Saturday being 'a bad day for obtaining buses'. Six copies of *The Land of Heart's Desire* were to be purchased at £2.2.0d. The competition for WI allotments was to be extended by having a class for Cottage Gardens which were defined as being those attached to houses and in which no paid labour is employed. Space was to be requested at the County Agricultural Show at Kettering and the next Produce Show would take place in 1931.

Before that a Handicraft Exhibition was held, this time with 870 entries from 70 WIs, the Challenge Urn being won by Duston, with Wootton 2nd and Pattishall 3rd. The scheduled Produce Show did in fact take place at Northampton Town Hall on 23rd September and was advertised as 'the first home, farm and garden exhibition and sale run by the WI', There were no fewer than 1,486 in the 70 classes, entries representing 58 institutes throughout the county. There was the keenest competition for the Institute prize given for the highest

---
* See photograph on page 199

The Northamptonshire County Federation of Women's Institutes.

Schedule of

Home, Farm and Garden EXHIBITION and SALE

Gift Stall of Produce for Federation Funds.

The Exhibition will be held at

The Town Hall, NORTHAMPTON,

ON

WEDNESDAY, SEPTEMBER 23rd, 1931.

Doors open 2.0 p.m.—7.0 p.m.

ADMISSION:—

Non-Members, 1/-. Members showing Badge or Membership Card, 6d.

Institute Secretaries may obtain Schedules for Members at 1d. each.

All correspondence connected with the Exhibition should be addressed to the

COUNTY SECRETARY, Raleigh Chambers,
St. Giles' Terrace, Northampton.

The first Home, Farm and Garden Exhibition and Sale notice, 1931.

number of marks This went to Wootton (with 34 members) who gained 104 points, with Harlestone runners-up.

The most popular class was that for fruit cake which attracted well over 100 entries, closely followed by home-made wine. Jam and plain cake also occasioned strong competition. Lady Knightley, in the absence of Countess Spencer who had recently undergone a slight operation, said she was pleased to see the members making their own bread. She hoped they all made it from National Mark flour! She also wished the members took a greater interest in their gardens. The men, although they must do the digging, could not be expected to do the whole of the gardening after a day's work. No matter how small the garden was, it should look as though someone loved it.

Later in the year it was reported Countess Spencer had attended a WI Exhibition at Oundle in the Victoria Hall. This was the first venture of such a kind attempted by a Group but it was obviously a huge success with 430 entries of an extraordinarily high standard. With both Produce and Handicraft classes the entries covered a very wide range and Lady Lilford in thanking Countess Spencer commented that when she came to the county over 30 years ago there was no such things as Women's Institutes, People made things and sent them to bazaars, but there was never anything suitable to buy. The advent of WIs had changed all that and the standard had improved out of all knowledge. And just to show nothing has ever changed, even then because Northamptonshire is such a long county, those WIs in the north did feel somewhat isolated and the comment was made that they wished Countess Spencer would come to their end of the county more often.

An At Home Propaganda meeting was held at Woodcock's Café in Peterborough in October at which Mrs. Nugent Harris spoke on the Aims and Objects of the WI. This was followed by an open discussion – 114 invitations had been sent out. Later meetings led to three more WIs being formed at Caistor, Marholm and Eye. If you have difficulty in recognising these names then it is because at this time we were still the County of Northamptonshire with the Soke of Peterborough.

At the Council Meeting held in the Lecture Room of the Free Library, Abington Street, Northampton on 10th December, 1931, 78 delegates attended in the morning and discussed the Schedule for the 1932 Produce Show and the National Mark Flour Cookery Competition. The speaker was from the Society for the Protection of Ancient Buildings, and trophies and certificates were awarded to the winners of the Dramatic Competitions held in November with Bars going to the Guild of Learners members.

It was at this meeting that Lady Knightley was presented with a dressing case on her resignation as County President which post she had held since the beginning of the Federation in 1920. The ballot for her successor resulted in the Countess Spencer, Brington, being elected. Two new members of Executive were Miss Schilizzi, Loddington, and Mrs Raynsford, Milton. Mrs. Gawthropp was leaving the county and so resigned and her place on the County Council Library committee was taken by Miss Luddington.

As has been mentioned, all committee meetings were held on Saturdays but it was now decided that although the day would remain the same the timings would alter with Music & Drama at 10.30 am (History had been dropped from the title), Organisation at 11.30 and Executive at 12 noon. This must tell us something about how to organise meetings with all of them taking so little time!

1932 began again with Miss Bouverie Chairman, Mrs. Renton Vice-Chairman, Mrs. Pelham from the Soke of Peterborough (co-opted). Mrs. Angus Ferguson, Elton, also became a member of the committee and was appointed representative to the County Library. Miss Simpson continued with her WI officers' conferences and held one in March with Mrs. Raynsford VCO speaking in the morning and Miss Eunson, County Treasurer in the afternoon.

This was followed on 9th April with the County's exciting drama production *Prunella* by A.E. Houseman, which was staged at the Repertory Theatre in Northampton, and the Music & Drama committee was congratulated on this performance. Takings £68.6s.4d. profit £23.7s.7d. At the Executive Committee in April members were told that Lady Knightley would be leaving the county, and within a period of months they were sadly sending a letter of sympathy to her on the death of her husband.

The Half-Yearly Council meeting on 20th April discussed the rural water supply survey and the possibility of publishing a County Cookery Book The report on the survey was given by the county secretary in the absence of the Medical Officer of Health. Entrants had been asked to write an essay on their particular supply from the housewife's point of view. 90 institutes sent in plans and completed questionnaires and 25 essays were submitted. The prize was won by a member of Dodford with Miss Edith Palmer of Gt. Oakley second.

Regarding the Recipe Book which it eventually became, as was expected, the members greeted this idea enthusiastically, so a separate committee was set up to compile this. The members of Executive were asked to guarantee £5 each if the publication was not a success and

Wicken, 1928.

3,000 copies were printed at £75. Mrs Steward, Brigstock, was Chairman of this committee and one of her recipes appears – Mint Jelly for Cold Mutton: Cover 3 lbs of gooseberries with water. Boil till soft and strain through a sieve. Allow 1 lb of sugar to a pint of juice and add a bunch of mint. Boil 20 minutes or until set. Take out the mint and put the jelly in small pots. The Book cost 6d. and there was never any need to take up the guarantees as it sold extremely well, and Second, Third and Fourth editions were published in due course.

Before undertaking this project Mrs. Steward who was a Cookery Judge and became Brigstock's President in 1928, produced her own cookery book 'How I Make my Jam', This book not only contained proof of the quality of the preserve but also home-spun philosophy on thrift. The proof of the quality was the certificate presented to her in 1931 by National which is on page 1 of the book. Her advice on thrift is shown below and we have to remember when this was written: 'Having had a home to manage for over thirty years, and always being interested in jam-making, I have gained a lot of knowledge from experience, which is not to be belittled as a teacher. When speaking at WI meetings I am often confronted with the remark 'We can't afford to buy a lot of sugar for jam when our husbands have a farm labourer's wage of 30s. per week'. I then tell them of a story on thrift which was told to me by a WI member. She said 'My husband earns 30s. per week and I make all my own jam. I buy a pound of sugar every week, at three pence halfpenny and put it away in a cupboard, and you can't buy a pound of jam for that price! If I can spare the money some weeks I buy two pounds.' All the garden that member had was a small patch in front of her cottage. They had a rhubarb bed and a marrow bed. She made various kinds of rhubarb jam, with lemon, ginger, oranges and blackberry and apple, as she used fallen apples given her from the farm and gathered the blackberries herself. 'Then I always make some dried apricot jam but that's my best jam; we only have that on Sundays or if we have company. At the end I can generally spare a little from my sugar store to make a little home-made wine.'

In the afternoon of 20th April the Handicraft Exhibition was held with an entry of 1064 from 64 WIs which showed 'a great improvement and was generally considered high, and the lecture good'. Some of the judges' remarks were 'much to be learnt in finishing edges' on rugs; 'uneven and crooked tucks' on gloves; 'design was the weak point' on banners and leatherwork. These were only a few of the classes so criticisms on the whole were sympathetic, suggesting that members probably needed a few more lessons in some techniques. A profit of £12. 15. 0d. was made which was thought to be satisfactory.

Voice production and singing classes held by Mrs Schilizzi at Loddington Hall had been much enjoyed and it was agreed classes for conductors should be held in May. Still with Mrs. Schilizzi, a Shakespearean Party was to be held at her home on 30th June. A café was to supply tea at 1s, per head, 2d. to be donated to the Federation.

King's Sutton, 1929.

Bus used for outings, 1929.

The play to be performed was *As You Like It* and reserved seats were charged at 2s in the afternoon, 6d. at night – all others 3d.

An Exhibition and Sale of Work had been held the week following the Half-Yearly Council meeting. This was a week long sale held at the Town Hall covering all arts and crafts and a press report stated the exhibited work would have done credit to many professional experts 'The impression of rural life assigned to the urban dweller must have been one of utter deprivation and boredom because it was also reported that the WI movement continued to grow as it had during the post war years, and with its present enthusiastic leadership and following it would not be long before the urban women's erstwhile attitude of tolerant superiority towards her rural sister would have to

Hargrave WI – Skegness outing, 1930.

Sale of Work, 1932 – Lady Northampton, Miss Clare, Miss Henman (judge), Lady Sybil Smith (judge), Mrs. Hobson, Mrs. Dobson (judge) and Mrs. Gordon Renton.

be radically revised'. It was felt that the value of the WI's activities as a relief from the monotony of country life, especially in winter, could not be over-estimated. Drama Area Festivals were organised to take place in six centres at, Guilsborough, Oundle, Daventry, Brackley, Wellingborough and Northampton with the Finals at Northampton. At the end of this Festival it was decided that in future there would only be four Area Festivals with no Final.

As a matter of economy for 1932 it was decided there should be no donation to the County Musical Competition, no tent at the Agricultural Show and no prizes for the County Show. Other than this, events continued in the normal pattern with a Produce Exhibition and Sale at the County Show at Rushden, and a Rally and Sale of Work at Delapre. The Annual Council Meeting's speaker was Miss Digby from National on the subject of Market Stalls, and as you will see later, in common with most Council Meetings then, the talks given at these times usually led to action being taken by the County Executive committee.

So this year Mrs. Barker's salary was increased to £150 and her assistant – a Miss Barker – received £60 They both lived at the same address so one assumes they were mother and daughter. A new duplicator was required and it was thought the committee table was too big. The office hours were listed as Wednesday 10.30 – 12 noon and Saturday, 10.30 – 1 pm and 2 – 4 pm. Following Miss Digby's talk on Market Stalls, a Market Conference was organised but was poorly attended – only 24 members from 14 WIs. Miss Cox, the National Markets Organiser explained the various procedures for setting up a stall, stating the importance of the Controller and the Treasurer. A village secretary should be appointed in each village who would supply a complete list of senders and their produce each week, also to collect produce and grade – all stuff to be fresh, clean and attractive to look at.

Money to start the stall would need to be borrowed from private people, 1d. in 1s. left as commission and the stall should be open not only to WI members but to stallholders, small farmers, etc. In answer to a question, Miss Cox stated market stalls were proving a success so far. The biggest business that year had been £3,000, partly owing to ex-service men. One small wayside village market had taken £120 and a new one in Devon took £166 in 22 days.

Controllers were usually paid from 5/6d to 7/6d per day and Treasurers were usually honorary. The County Federation would call the first meeting to consider a stall, and this is in fact what happened in Northamptonshire when an ad hoc committee was set up with a view to reporting early in 1934 so that the question of a stall could come to the 1935 Council Meeting.

The Half-Yearly Council Meeting was held in May 1933 with 161 members attending from 71 WIs and the talk was on Finance. In September a Produce Show was held in the Town Hall with 71 classes. Must have been something magical about the number 71 that year, but without going into too much detail the consequent report in the local newspaper ran into three full page columns. The winners in every class were listed as well as the organisers and those members of Executive who had attended.

Two conferences took place in October, the first a combined Handicraft one at Banbury with Oxfordshire which Lady Spencer opened. The profit received from this was £12.12.0d which was divided equally between the two counties. The second was at Peterborough when Mrs. Winteringham from National spoke on the WI and Public Life, followed by Mrs. Munro, a National member from Leicestershire, who spoke on National and County Federations. November saw the Drama, Music and Dancing sub-committee organising their annual Festival when the judge Miss Henzie Raeburn spoke on The Place of the Producer in Drama. This was held in St. Crispin's Hall in

Novices Handicraft Exhibition, 1934 – Miss Clarke, Mrs. Renton, Mrs. Eunson, Mrs. Cooke, Mrs. Hobson.

Northampton over two days. Crick won a First Class Certificate for *Two Blind Men and a Donkey* and a Third Class one for *The Spinsters of Lushe*. Guilsborough also won a Third Class Certificate for *What do you Think?* Crick's first play Miss Raeburn thought was great fun. It was a big job for the producer but it had been well done and the vitality was lovely. Commenting on one of the plays she said 'it is dangerous to have a live animal on the stage'. In this case it was a dog and the audience watched him and forgot the players!

There were problems at this time with copyright for the performance of certain plays in WIs. Duston were to be sued by Samuel French who insisted that a performance at a WI monthly meeting at which more than 30 members were present could not be called a private performance. National were contacted and a young Stafford Cripps was engaged as Counsel. However, no action was taken against the WI.

Mrs. Mordaunt, Castle Ashby, was appointed to National's Music and Drama sub-committee this year.

The year ended with the Council Meeting in December with Mrs. Pickersgill as speaker. 31 members had stood for election and it was good to see that Mrs. Pelham of Castor and Mrs. Angus Ferguson of Ecton, both from the Soke of Peterborough had been elected. The

Marchioness of Northampton had also become a committee member, much to the delight of the members. Although Miss Bouverie was allowed by her doctor to take the chair at this meeting she was not allowed to speak.

Into 1934 with a Novices Handicraft Exhibition being held in April, Lady Northampton to present the prizes. The profit from this was £13.15.3d. but in the February newsletter Groups had been asked to make a special effort regarding fundraising which led to one irate President writing in to deplore the continuous request for funds, saying that the Federation should work within its means and cut back the amount of work undertaken.

Mrs. Capel, Old Stratford, pillow lace making.

The Half-yearly Council Meeting was held in the morning of 2nd May when there were 7 resolutions and Miss Cowlin from Bristol spoke on The Children's Act. A resolution was asking for that particular meeting to be held occasionally on a Saturday rather than Wednesday, and further that it should be held in the afternoon as most ordinary WI members were fully occupied in their own homes in the mornings.

A Presidents and Vice-Presidents Conference was held in the afternoon with over 100 attending. when a great deal of valuable advice had been given by the various speakers.

Reports were given of the National Annual General Meeting, and those of Lady Spencer were excellent being easy to read and very concise, and it was at the 1934 one – the 18th – that John Simon, the Secretary of State for Foreign Affairs spoke about everyone working for international peace. The remark was made that 'men build houses, women build homes'. Apparently three Northamptonshire members started an exodus before lunch, having been specifically asked to stay in their seats. They were reprimanded from the Chair by Lady Denman who said she also wanted her lunch as much as they did!

The Northamptonshire Agricultural Show at Kettering featured an Exhibition of Produce and Handicrafts and a handsome scarf in the 'goose eye' pattern was presented to the Prince of Wales. The Federation later received a letter of thanks from the Prince, and talking about farming at the Show he said he wished to deal with two points in particular. 'One is this very distressed industry in which I am engaged in the West of England and the other the drought that is worrying all of us so much at the present time ... I was so pleased to see in the Women's Institute tent demonstrations of the best way of packing fruit and vegetables.' There were in fact 159 entries for the Show, of which 44 received 1st class Certificates.

This was the first year the Federation had appeared at the Peterborough Show. It was a great success and for a first attempt in that district the Exhibit was very good indeed. There were 267 entries. 111 first class certificates were awarded, 67 second class and 40 third. The special co- operative prizes were won by Glinton and Warmington with 98% each for Produce and Castor and Warmington with 100% each for Handicraft. Miss Healey of Warmington was the individual winner for the highest number of marks at the Show.

A Council Meeting was held at Peterborough in October 1934 with Countess Spencer in the chair. There were approximately 100 members present at the morning session and in the afternoon Mrs. Raynsford talked about the social half-hour. It was during this year that Miss Simpson wrote a book about Games for Playing in WI social time. Regarding this Council Meeting held at Peterborough it was agreed in future to call it a Conference as there can only be one Annual General Meeting of the Federation and that was always held in Northampton.

Year end again and the December Annual Meeting featured five resolutions 1) that the election of the Executive Committee shall take place in future by postal ballot; 2) that at future county Agricultural Shows no exhibits shall be removed from the WI tent until 4 pm on the second day of the show; 3) that in 1935 the annual effort for county funds should take the form of a Sale and Entertainment inside a suitable building, rather than a Garden Fete dependent for its success on the clemency of the weather; 4) that the National Gardens Guild Bulb Competition should be organised through the County office; and

5) that the Annual Meeting of the National Federation should be preceded, preferably on the previous day, by a business meeting which should be attended by a limited number of delegates each representing more than one WI; that the Annual Meeting should take the shape of a Rally open to all members, together with Resolutions and Speeches on topics of general interest. Members, or their WIs to be responsible for their own expenses. The meeting finished with a short entertainment by the Music, Drama and Dancing Committee. This took the form of a charade with such things as a sack race, one member blowing a tin trumpet and waving a toy shrieker, finishing with the whole of the committee in a Noah's Ark scene in which they wore long white garments, carried umbrellas and complained loudly of 'the damp'. Lady Henley had a perpetual cold, sneezing with great enthusiasm – to the delight of the audience.

The List of Demonstrators and Speaker was to be discussed at a Council Meeting and then revised, and as the County was to enter the National Handicraft Competition for a Co-operative effort, in this case a Loan Collection, the idea was revised and WIs were to be asked to submit specimens for the Collection – they were to be simple but perfect.

Early in 1935 Miss Bouverie announced her retirement as a VCO and many letters of appreciation were received from the WIs. This was sad news for everyone, but in other respects 1935 had been a year of celebration with the Jubilee of King George V and Queen Mary.

Following an earlier production of *Prunella* the Drama, Music and Dancing committee turned their attention to *The Trojan Women*, performing it at the Rugby Co-operative Hall, the Northampton Repertory Theatre and the Kettering Co-operative Hall, during a fortnight in October. The translation from the original by Euripedes was by Professor Gilbert Murray, the Greek scholar who gifted his royalties to the League of Nations Union. They were obviously a very talented committee as full houses were reported at all venues. The committee also entered various British Drama League competitions with some degree of success.

Going into 1936, although the original concept of the WI was to concentrate on produce and help with the rural economy, we have so far launched into a Handicraft Guild with many Shows and Exhibitions being held to show the WI skills in this field. Drama, too, seems to have been very much in favour, but following on from the Victorians maybe this is not surprising as families were used to providing their own entertainment. However, Produce was not

Drama Festival, 1935 – St Crispin's Northampton. Gt. & Lt. Oakley – Tap three Times.

Rose Pageant, September 1935 – Kings and Queens of England.

Lady Henley, Watford.

entirely neglected with Produce Shows and Exhibits at both the County and Peterborough Shows; then there were the Gardens competitions. However, we are now leading up to the Second World War, and we will see what develops. Northamptonshire by this time has 144 WIs with 7379 members.

Chapter 5
THINKING GLOBALLY
1936–1944

Although we did not know it at the time the world was edging nearer and nearer to World War II with all its implications for women on the home front, but before that the WI itself was looking towards more peaceful happenings. Have you ever wondered over the past decade what happened to Mrs Madge Watt who had been instrumental in getting WIs started in both Wales and England?. You may remember that from 1915 onwards Mrs. Watt continued with her work as WI Organiser until 1917 when the Agricultural Organisation Society appointed Lady Denman to become Chairman of the WI sub-committee and later the National Chairman of the Women's Institutes. Mrs. Watt herself began to look further afield to continue her work as she felt there could be an international organisation to help women the world over in rural areas. She shared this dream with two other women who worked tirelessly towards making this dream a reality. They were the Marchioness of Aberdeen and Temair, LL.D., JP. who was President of the International Council of Women, and Miss Elsie Zimmern, a child welfare specialist. It was at a meeting of the ICW in Geneva in 1927 that discussion turned to the possibility of an international conference for women. So it was that, with these three intrepid women organising affairs, this conference took place on 30th April 1929 when delegates from 24 countries came together in London over four days to discuss shared experiences, describing their daily lives and airing their views on education, health, economics, family and social life, only to find many common threads.

The conference was a huge success, coming as it did only one year after the Equal Franchise Act had given full voting rights to women in the United Kingdom. At the end of the conference a Liaison Committee was formed and was given a small budget and space in ICW's offices in London. It was chaired by Mrs. Watt, with Miss E.H. Pratt. Women's agricultural education officer at the Ministry of Agriculture, Vice-Chairman and Miss Zimmern as Honorary Secretary.

The Vienna Conference in 1930 was attended by delegates from twenty-eight countries who decided to carry on with this informal association of countrywomen and hold a further conference at Stockholm in 1933. Both conferences were very successful and the one in Vienna is now considered the first ACWW Triennial Conference. It was at this conference that it was agreed to open a central headquarters in London. A small one-roomed office was found at 26 Eccleston Square. Miss Zimmern, who was the practical and efficient member of the team set about equipping and furnishing this office, bringing along her own typewriter to deal with correspondence. Mrs. Watt was a stirring speaker and a passionate promoter of the association's aims. Together they made contact with like-minded women's organisation all over the world.

A letter was received from Finland telling of the work of Finnish country people and because it was so interesting it was decided to copy this and send it to other organisations. This was the beginning of 'Links of Friendship' a successful monthly mailing from Central Office.

Before the Stockholm Conference took place a first Annual Business Meeting was held in May 1931 when twenty-eight countries were represented. A roll of 100 donors of £5 was inaugurated and individual contributing members were enrolled at a subscription of £1 per annum. Three new committees were set up – Finance chaired by Mrs. Godfrey Drage, MBE, JP, and Constitution and Agenda, both chaired by Miss Pratt.

In Stockholm 1933 an association of rural women's societies was formed with Mrs. Watt unanimously elected President and eight vice-presidents being elected from different parts of the world – America, Gt. Britain, Australia, Germany, France, Norway, South Africa and Ceylon. A constitution was presented and adopted, the objects of which were:

1) to promote and maintain friendly and helpful relations between the country women's and homemakers' associations of all nations and to give any possible help in their development;
2) to further the common interests of these organisations in the economic, social and cultural spheres, while avoiding political and sectarian questions of a controversial nature;
3) to encourage the formation of organisations working for such common interests in countries where this need had not already been met.

The most dramatic and significant moment in the meeting came when

Mrs. Watt strode to the blackboard and wrote the following words: ASSOCIATED COUNTRYWOMEN OF THE WORLD. She was followed by the German, the Swiss and Swedish delegates writing the same words in their own particular languages. And thus ACWW was born. Lady Aberdeen had said at that time that the greatest challenge for the next few years was to find ways to achieve its ambitions with only the most meagre of resources to sustain it. This is when Mrs. Drage suggested that each member should contribute a penny a year in addition to the official dues paid by societies. This idea was launched in 1936 as the Million Member Fund and soon became known as 'Pennies for Friendship' This money is still collected to-day and forms the major part of ACWW's income.

Nationally a major constitutional problem was the non-party political character of the WI which Lady Denman believed to be

The ACWW badge symbolises the four points of the compass linked together by a circle of friendship against a green background, representing the earth's green carpet. It was designed by Madge Watt's son, Robin Watt MC.

so important. Her words on this are as true today as they were in 1935 – 'In the first place we must accept the fact that almost every question is either party political or sectarian. If we shirk this difficult task, and discourage WIs from discussing anything which might give rise to party political or sectarian issues, or if we discourage WIs from discussing anything which might lead to difficulties we shall limit ourselves to trivialities and do irreparable harm to our movement'. What an inspirational leader she was, and action on all kinds of issues do attract young women of today to join the ranks of the WI.

Remembering our history, 1936 was the year King George V died, to be followed by the abdication of Edward VIII and the subsequent Coronation of King George VI, all momentous happenings. Television programmes were first broadcast from Alexandra Palace in this year,

Cranford Choral Society, 1936 – winners of Lady Violet Brassey Cup at Oundle. Mrs. George Brudenell is holding the Cup.

but my memory is only of hearing the news on the 'wireless' with very sombre music being played on the death of King George V.

Regarding King George V, a resolution was passed at the May 1936 Council Meeting ' that the membership supported the proposal that Cottages and Flats for the Aged, where some provision is made for assistance and supervision during illness and infirmity, should form a National Memorial to King George V, and asks the Lord Mayor of London to give the scheme his fullest consideration'. A copy of Northamptonshire's letter to the Lord Mayor following this meeting is available in the Records, but there is no mention of a reply.

As far as the Federation was concerned, 1936 saw the acquisition of 160 percussion instruments for the use of committee members when visiting WIs. The WI had to pay to hire them and any out of pocket expenses for committee members were also to be paid. Later in the year it was reported that two dulcimers at 2/6d. each and a triangle at 5s. had been added to the instruments.

The Federation was wishing to move to new offices so two rooms at the Ladies Club in Marefair were looked at, one to be a lock-up office and the other a large committee room for meetings, conferences, etc. The rental was £52 per year to include light and heat, so the move was made. Executive and Organisation changed their meeting days to Wednesday, at 11 am and 2.15 respectively, and to this day they both still meet on a Wednesday, but now separated by two weeks!

There was a shortfall in the County budget of £100, so in addition to the Tennis Tournament to be held at Loddington it was decided to have a Fete and Concert, which did in fact result in a profit of £73.

Council meetings continued to be held, and the Music and Drama committee decided to separate and look after their specific interests. In 1937 the Federation entered the British Drama League competition with their rendering of *The House Fairies* and were the winners. The speaker at the May meeting was on the Preservation of Rural England, and by the end of the year, after yet one more Rally and a Whist Drive, and a discussion on raising funds at the Half-Yearly Council meeting, letters were received asking the County to consider curtailing activities, wishing to have fewer events with the large Shows and Rallies occurring only every 2/3 years, rotating drama handicrafts and produce. A further WI wrote to say the members felt increasingly sad at being scolded for not raising large sums of money more willingly.

Coronation year saw members being encouraged to plant at least one tree to commemorate the occasion. A great many were planted, and this has become a major tradition in WIs, with trees being planted to celebrate numerous occasions. Weedon and Cogenhoe gave seats to their respective villages and Ecton 24 chairs to the parish hall. Preston Capes formed a committee with some of the village men and raised enough money to give free teas to the adults and children and also a mug to the children. Later they intended to give a bus shelter to the village. Guilsborough joined in the village collections and the surplus money formed a fund for a Playing Field. Most of the WIs helped with teas, sports, etc. in their villages.

This year also saw Lady Spencer being congratulated on her appointment as Lady-in-Waiting to the Queen.

The Half-yearly Council Meeting was held in April 1937 in the Town Hall, Northampton when the WIs exhibited the flowers from the bulbs that had been distributed to them by the County. Crick were the winners in the Narcissus class and East Haddon the Daffodils. It was at this meeting that a Rural Community Council was suggested for Northamptonshire but it was felt there was no need for one at that time. The Agriculture and Horticulture committee organised a reprint of the Recipe Book, the third edition which was somewhat enlarged,

Tree planting, 1937 – to mark the Coronation of George VI.

and 2000 were ordered at a cost of £45. An Open Day at Moulton Farm Institute was organised which 400 members, families and friends attended.

At the Annual General Meeting in December it was reported that a Produce Show had been held at Kettering where a Cook's Corner had been popular. There had also been a Sweet Stall and Ice Creams and the demonstrations had been on Packing and Grading for exhibitions. It had been agreed that the Tent this year should be for Publicity and Display only. At this meeting we first hear of Mrs. Tynan of Isham being elected to Executive, and a further committee – **PUBLIC QUESTIONS, HEALTH and EDUCATION** – being appointed. Membership of Executive had increased from 12 to 15. This meeting ended with the Percussion Band performing with community singing, and later a Morality Play.

1937, too, was National's 21st Anniversary and each County was asked to produce a page to be presented to Lady Denman. Northamptonshire felt a celebration should not be held this year but should wait until the 25th Anniversary. However, National stated that having started the ball rolling they felt they should go through with it. Northamptonshire's design for the Denman Page depicted a decorative map showing the WIs of the members of Executive, with various symbols of activities in the County around this – bootmakers, hunting, agriculture, handicrafts.

Two members of Executive had the opportunity to view the completed book and described it as 'charming and original' and they hoped all WI members would have an opportunity to see it, possibly at a Produce Show.

Regarding the Coronation, Northamptonshire were allocated 13 seats for the Procession and these had to be ballotted for amongst the 147 WIs. The final list accepting places was Brington, Chelveston, Blatherwyck, Ecton, Welford, Wilbarston and Stoke Albany, Braunston, Weekly and Warkton, Caistor, Badby, Wootton and Grafton Underwood.

Physical Culture was the topical subject and featured at the Council meeting, so here we see the beginnings of so-called sporting activities. A Quota system was also discussed; if the suggested 1/3d was paid by each WI this would amount to £446.15.0d leaving about £30 to be raised by some smaller event. This was agreed.

Reported Lady Nunburnholme, Arthingworth, appointed to National Music sub-committee, and Miss Bouverie was congratulated on being awarded an OBE.

However, before getting ahead too far, I need now to update you as to what has been happening with WI Markets. As already mentioned we had Miss Digby speaking from National at one of the Council Meetings and Miss Vera Cox, the National Markets Adviser had also spoken. An ad hoc committee had considered all the implications of markets in Northamptonshire.

Markets were first set up in 1919 to provide a service to the community by bringing fresh homegrown produce from the garden and kitchen and crafts from the country for sale in towns, the first one being started in Lewes, in East Sussex. From the outset WI Markets helped not only WI members, but unemployed people, pensioners and ex-servicemen who had no other means of disposing of surplus produce.

In 1932 a National Resolution pledged WI members to organise and increase the number of Markets. This is when the Markets Department of National was set up and Miss Vera Cox was appointed. Because the Constitution of the WI does not permit regular trading the Markets Department applied to the Carnegie Trust who asked NFWI to open Markets to non-WI Members both men and women. This has been the policy ever since. When the grant ceased, the Markets themselves agreed to a yearly contribution to the Markets Department based on turnover. This was set at 1%, the same as the original figure.

Throughout many changes in conditions the aims of Markets have been the same:

1) to help people to develop their skills and market their produce by working co-operatively
2) to make it worthwhile financially to cultivate their gardens
3) to prevent waste by encouraging good growth and harvesting
4) to encourage the practice of home skills

The standard of the Market goods is set by the Controller who works on behalf of the committee to check the quality, quantity and price as produce comes to the Market each week. The range of all the sections obviously depends on the people who get involved.

The link between the Markets and the County Federation is a VCMO, Voluntary County Marketing Organiser. Her duties involve being responsible for organising Markets and arranging training days for Market shareholders and WI members. She is a friend and adviser to the Markets and is regarded as an extension of the Markets committee.

To become a shareholder you pay the sum of five pence, which means you can sell your produce in any Market in that Society. The money taken on a weekly Market is paid back to the producer on a monthly basis less a commission which is decided by each Market at its Annual Meeting. The commission is used to pay for rent, insurance, audit, quotes and general expenses in the running of the Market.

Running alongside Markets there were the Produce Guilds. As you know, the Handicraft Guild had been in existence from the 1920s and it was always hoped that a similar venture would happen with regard to Produce. In 1938 Lady Denman was appointed Chairman of the National Produce Guild. She reported that a grant had been received from HM Treasury for the development of agricultural work. This grant would make it possible for Headquarters to employ an extra organiser whose first duty would be to help build up the National Guild. The members would have the opportunity of attending schools and studying, taking tests in various branches of agriculture and horticulture and in the use and presentation of home-made produce. This would all result in a body of experts who would be of the same value as the Guild of Learners had been to handicrafts.

An inaugural meeting to decide to form a Produce Guild, in conjunction with the Northamptonshire Federation of Women's Institutes, was held at Cottesbrooke Hall when 120 delegates attended. Mrs. Macdonald-Buchanan had agreed to be its Chairman. The following were committee members: Mrs. Leslie Church, Miss Corner and Mrs. A.G.Gilby, all of Spratton, Mrs. Gibbs of Harlestone, Mrs. Lance Baker of Oundle, Mrs. Wykeham of West Haddon, Miss Strang, dairy and poultry instructress at Moulton Institute of Agriculture, with

Miss M.D. Webster, Cottesbrooke, as secretary. Here we have the first mention of someone so many members will have met during the last 50 years – Mrs. Monicreff Dickens whose maiden name was Webster. One of her memories was the fact that she used to cycle a round eight miles to attend a WI and was most anxious to take part in most activities but not THE DRAMA, which apparently did not tempt her. Mrs. Dickens said that serving on a county committee began a most interesting period of her life. Money was scarce and even asking for a fee of five shillings was suspect and the amount of happy voluntary work that was done was unbelievable and this by members who had no electric gadgets, cookers, hot water systems but were very proud of belonging to 'the Institute'.

The decision to have a Northamptonshire Produce Guild was ratified at the May 1939 Half-Yearly Meeting. The objects of the Produce Guild were to interest and train members in agricultural and horticultural work, with district classes being arranged. Tests were to be held later and successful candidates would be awarded bars.

In the event of war, members of the Produce Guild would be required to undergo an intensive course in food production and conservation of food. Sections to be developed were gardening, poultry keeping, dairying, beekeeping, pig keeping, food preserving and cookery. Following this initial meeting, delegates were conducted by Mrs. Macdonald-Buchanan round the kitchen garden of Cottesbrooke Hall, where a demonstration was given by the head gardener, and also round the ornamental garden. Following meetings on 13th September at the home of Mrs. Lester Reid, Thorpe Mandeville, and on the 14th at the home of the Hon. Mrs. A.F.H. Ferguson of Polebrook, it was proposed that a County Rally should be held at the Moulton Institute of Agriculture.

The Guild pledged to encourage members to make the very best use of the ground and facilitate what they had available, not necessarily for sale but to supply themselves and their families and possible evacuees. The Ministry of Agriculture, realising the importance of the WI movement in relation to food production and preservation had promised an annual grant of £500, which sum would be taken up almost entirely by salary and expenses for the National Organiser. In the Spring of 1939 war seemed imminent and a letter from the County Council in April asked authorities to take such action as would be necessary for the training of the Women's Land Army should the need arise. The Women's Land Army was first created during World War One, when the women took over men's work on the farms. With so many young men being called up for the armed services there was a real gap in farm workers in the Second World War and so the system was resurrected. Women did all the jobs that were required to make a farm function, normally milking, threshing, ploughing, tractor driving, etc. Their wage, over 18, was £1.12 pence a week after deductions had been made for lodgings and food. The maximum working week was 50 hours in the summer and 48 hours in the winter. Lady Denman was appointed Honorary Director of the Women's Land Army and the Headquarters were based at her home at Balcombe Place in Sussex.. The uniform consisted of one green v-necked pullover, one fawn shirt, one pair of brown corduroy or whipcord breeches, a brown cowboy style hat, fawn knee length woollen socks and very hard brown brogues.

Two members from Northamptonshire, Jocelyn Woodville-Price from Easton & Collyweston and Audrey Allen of Bozeat have vivid memories of their time as Land Girls. Mainly they were allocated the early shift, getting up at 5 am and milking the cows, cleaning the dairy and cowsheds afterwards before going in for breakfast. Jocelyn tells of being so tired one day she found herself sitting down – half asleep having already milked six cows – and reaching for the cow's udders to find to her horror she was sitting near the bull. Fortunately he was too busy eating so she gently rose, breathed a sigh of relief and leaned against the wall curled up with laughter. Audrey said ' it was all hard physical work but very rewarding knowing that producing food was a vital part of the war effort'.

Land Girls quickly became accustomed to life on the farm and many stayed on in the countryside after the war. However, there were others who longed to get back to their own large cities and did so at the earliest opportunity.

A short course for Land Army volunteers was held in July 1939 at Moulton and with the outbreak of hostilities on 3rd September, all ordinary courses of instruction were cancelled. Eventually 1300 women were trained for the Women's Land Army. These courses were held regularly during the war and at the request of the Ministry of Agriculture all technical assistance was placed at the disposal of the County War Agricultural Executive Committee and every effort was made to encourage the work of the WI Produce Guild, Pig Clubs and the County Allotment holders in order to increase the home production of food. Miss Strang was awarded the MBE for her services, and it was through Miss Strang that the WI interest in home economics was developed. She was a representative member of the WI committee

P. G.

NATIONAL FEDERATION OF WOMEN'S INSTITUTES

PRODUCE GUILD

Membership Card
(WAR-TIME PERIOD)

Northamptonshire Soke of Peterborough
COUNTY FEDERATION

AIM: To encourage production and the best use, preservation and marketing of home-grown produce.

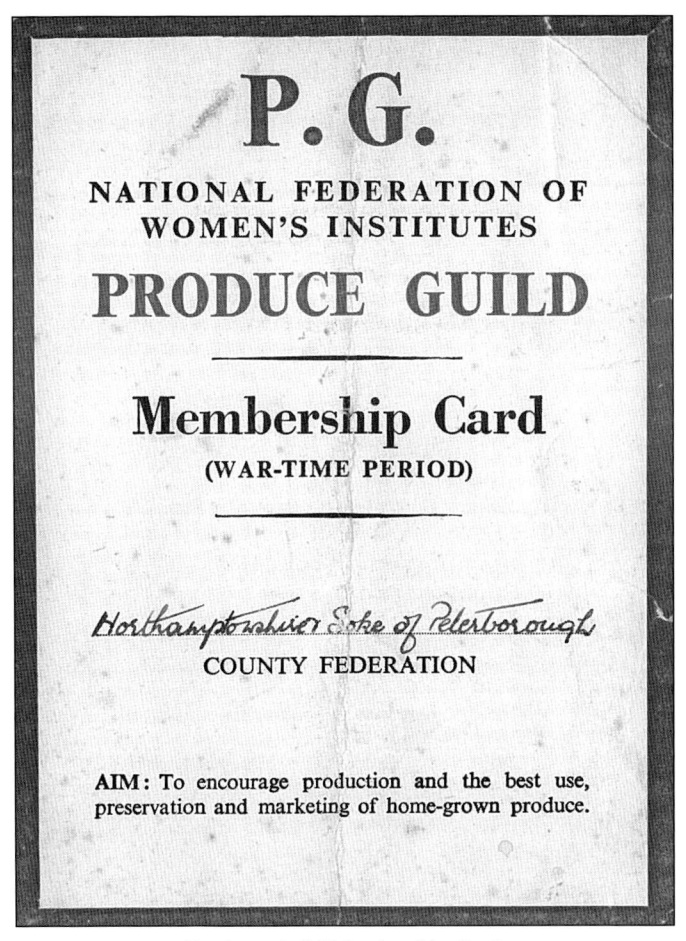

Produce Guild Membership Card.

and many classes were held at Moulton Agricultural College which the Farm Institute was to become.

For those women who were not able to leave their homes and had their families to look after, they helped the country in the war effort in a quiet way through the 'Dig for Victory' campaign, by the preserving of food, by helping with Air Raid Precautions and First Aid.

At the Peterborough Show in 1938 entries had been up by nearly 10% in the produce section but handicrafts had been down slightly, and the Show had produced a deficit of £5. 13. 4d.

Wartime transport to Group meeting.

The Annual Conference at Peterborough welcomed Miss Brocklebank, the National Federation Music Adviser and she had suggested a Leaders' School, one-day at each end of the county. There were several volunteer conductors and many members asking to sing.

A Questionnaire sent to WIs asking if they wished to have Keep Fit Classes and 17 replied in the affirmative.

Again in 1938, the Half Yearly Council Meeting was a great success with Miss Grace Hadow speaking on 'Ourselves as Citizens' and it left members with a feeling of responsibility to help others whenever possible. At the December Annual Meeting, Lady Denman had reported that there were 5,470 WIs nationally with 328,000 members. The number of Voluntary County Organisers had risen to 450, who had made 7,047 visits to WIs. However, she did say that we all knew there were still villages without adequate supplies of water, there were schools which were a disgrace, there were houses which should have been re-conditioned or pulled down years ago, there were thousands of women still suffering unnecessary pain in childbirth, and there were children growing up without adequate milk. She felt that of all these things there was not one of them that the united efforts of 380,000 women could not and should not cure.

A year later, on 3rd September 1939 it was announced that Britain was at war with Germany. Two days before the Government had issued an Evacuation Order whereby children under the age of 14 would be sent either to the countryside or abroad, wherever it was considered to be safe. Billeting in chosen areas of the country was compulsory and fines were imposed on anyone refusing to take evacuees. They were sent off from city areas with gas masks and luggage labels giving their names and the names of their schools. 10/6d. was the amount allowed for one child to be looked after, 8/6d.for each child if there was more than one, 5s. for an adult, water and sanitation given, accommodation (perhaps use of kitchen) – not board – being provided. When arriving at their new destination they were taken to a communal eating place, e.g. village hall, parish hall or school and were literally chosen by their new 'parent/s'. mainly for their usefulness. Having travelled across country in trains with no toilet facilities, or food, they were extremely hungry and dirty and must have been a pitiful sight. Brothers, sisters, etc. were split up, some being very lucky and looked after well, others really having to do a great deal of work in their new homes. Mothers often came too but were described as lazy, not being used to cooking or cleaning, but being smokers and having a liking for drink – very much a generalisation.

WI members were, of course, very much involved with taking in evacuees and three months after the September evacuation the National Federation issued a questionnaire to every WI asking for particulars of the adults and children received in their village. Careful instructions were sent out with the questionnaire. The accompanying letter said: 'The earlier reports as to the condition and habits of a small section of evacuees were of a distressing kind, but it is now being said that such reports were greatly exaggerated. Your committee feels that it would be a constructive piece of work if the institutes can give an accurate picture of the condition of the mothers and children when they arrived in the villages. If this is done while the events are still clear in our minds it will be of great value to the authorities who are responsible for the social conditions and health education of the community. Such a survey would not be undertaken in a spirit of grievance but as a definite contribution to the welfare of our fellow citizens'.

The Government expressed its gratitude to WI members when they turned to them for help in the September crisis regarding evacuation. The scheme had been rushed through at short notice but members responded nobly. A survey of the homes of some 16 million people had taken place prior to the evacuation. It was estimated that 3,000 children would reach each receiving point. Adults accompanying would be one in 10 and not higher than 1 in 20.

In Northamptonshire letters were sent to WIs asking whether they favoured the idea of a communal eating centre for school children who were billeted on them, in which case the WVS would help organise this if it was thought necessary.

A centralised scheme was organised by the Red Cross, St. John's Ambulance Association, the Women's Voluntary Service and the WI, to co-ordinate and work on behalf of the sick and wounded soldiers who might be sent to Northamptonshire. The initial steps were taken towards forming an organisation to embrace the whole of the county, the provision of comforts for soldiers other than those serving overseas also being included.

The Half-Yearly Council Meeting held in April 1939 in the Town Hall, Northampton was attended by 113 delegates. One of the speakers was Mr. Francis of the British Electrical Development Association. This was a follow-up to a resolution proposed at an earlier meeting when it had been decided to ask an expert for an explanation of the practical and financial side of the rural distribution of electricity before pressing for immediate action to provide electricity in all country areas. Mr. Francis explained that at that time there was hardly a rural centre in the country with a population of over 400 that was without electricity. Experimental rural development began in 1929 and during the next ten years had been fairly rapid. In rural districts development costs were high while potential revenue was low; nevertheless practically two-thirds of all the premises in rural areas were either connected up or were within reach of an electricity supply. Town and country electrification represented two different problems. In towns there was a mains in every street and a house could be connected simply by running a short length of cable from the main. There were no way leave difficulties nor was it necessary to install sub-stations for stepping down the voltage as was the case in rural areas. The further development of electricity in the countryside depended on two factors – the first in the hands of the consumers themselves – the more they used electricity the more the cost was likely to come down. The second was that of finance and depended on the possibility of attracting capital for that purpose.

A Produce Show was held in May 1939 and a letter from Lady Cynthia Spencer, the County President, asked for contributions to a Cook's Corner which had been popular at a similar show in 1937. It was explained that a Cook's Corner was a gift stall for food ready to be served or only requiring re-heating. 'The gift should be home made by

*Delegates to the Annual Council Meeting, Northampton 1939.
Lady Cynthia Spencer (inset left).*

either the President, Vice-President or her cook. Any dish will be acceptable, from a Milk Pudding to a Raised Pie, Cake, Brawn or Cooked Fowl. Each gift should be labelled with donor's name, and the interest would be heightened if recipes were included or a list of ingredients were added.

By November 1939 Northamptonshire Executive had had sufficient time to consider the future and had issued proposals for the curtailment of County Federation work. The policy suggested for 1940 was to hold the AGM in January 1940 instead of December 1939.

Regarding sub-committees, Drama was to suspend all activities, Handicrafts to dispense with regular meetings and confine committee work to co-operation with the WVS in regard to handwork to be done for the Red Cross and comforts for the troops – all statistics of the work done by individual members and WIs co-operatively to be kept by the County Secretary; Organisation was to hold meetings when matters of importance arose, preferably in a member's house. The Produce Guild was to hold the full number of meetings and to combine activities with the Agriculture and Horticulture committees; Headquarters to close the Northampton office – equipment to be stored in a committee member's house, the appointment of the Assistant Secretary to be discontinued; the Secretary to be encouraged to concentrate her work in two mornings and one afternoon a week, and to encourage the use of her telephone during the morning hours to save time and secretarial work; the Monthly Letter was to be suspended and visits of VCOs and County Federation members were to be curtailed, except in cases of emergency or real difficulty; the Treasurer would budget the expenditure for 1940 to meet the affiliation fee with a small working balance.

These proposals were sent to National and a reply received saying they deprecated such a policy being adopted. 'Though we must all realise the need for economy, there is on the other hand quite clearly an important field of work for the WIs in wartime and it is only through efficient organisation that their contribution to the national effort can be made effective.' They hoped very much that the committee would not feel it advisable to adopt the suggested policy. Northamptonshire obviously took notice of National's wish.

Also in November 1939 a Conference was held in Oxford which Miss Grace Hadow chaired; this was called to consider wartime programmes, how best to discover and develop local talent, and to improve co-operation between neighbouring Federations. Miss Hadow thought there was a tendency to overestimate the effects of the blackout in the country and the difficulties of transport. She felt there were certain advantages to be gained if WIs had to rely on local talent and their own members for their programmes. She thought the most important work that the Federations could undertake was to encourage and train this local talent. Speakers parties should be organised within reach of County boundaries.

A restricted Annual Meeting was held in December 1939 at 33 Marefair attended by Executive members, VCOs, sub-committee members and Group Conveners. There were 33 members present in all and discussion took place on the 1940 programme for WIs. It was reported that each sub-committee was drawing up plans to help WIs with their programme. Groups Conveners were asked to get in touch with their Presidents and Secretaries with a view to arranging for speakers for the WIs in their Group.

Miss Digby spoke on International Relations and Letter Friends suggesting that an International speaker should be appointed to the Public Questions committee. This was obviously the beginning of Northamptonshire's support for ACWW and each WI was eventually asked to appoint an international representative to collate all information sent to WIs on this subject. Letter friends were also the beginning of twinning of WIs in Northamptonshire with others around the world, and many maintain these contacts to-day.

In the event, as far as individual WIs were concerned social functions were continued, but full programmes would only be resumed when it was definitely established that the crisis was over. One of the biggest problems was the question of the blackout, because although meetings were generally held in the afternoons, it was dark before they ended so consideration had to be paid to ensuring the blackout facilities were adequate in all meeting places.

A further conference was to be held in March 1940 in Oxford for leaders of inter-county parties, the resulting schools to be reserved for those who needed training and not just for observers. For every party there should be at least two teachers and 20 would be a good number to be trained. Agendas should include voice production, how to keep the attention of audiences, how to prepare and present talks, suitable subjects and do's and don'ts. Speaking parties should be arranged between April and July 1940 and names of hostesses should be brought to the March meeting – evacuated teachers to be asked if they could help.

Following this meeting, Leaders' schools for speakers were organised for the Bedfordshire boundary at Bedford which Mrs.

Tynan, Mrs. J.P. Brown, Mrs. Downing and Mrs. Sitwell attended and for Leicestershire at East Carlton attended by Mrs. Angus Ferguson and Mrs. Wilkinson. These were very successful, so further meetings were arranged at Sulgrave, Old Stratford, Cranford and Duddington.

In 1940 also it was sadly reported that Miss Grace Hadow, National Vice-Chairman had died and much of her work was carried on by Miss Nancy Tennant. Miss Hadow had been a member of National Executive since 1934 and became National Vice-Chairman in 1940, in which capacity she served until 1948 under both Lady Denman and Lady Albemarle.

The Treasurer suggested a reduced budget for 1940 of £455 as opposed to £493 in 1939, cheaper paper and envelopes being one means of saving. The Quota was to be reduced by 1d. to 1/1d. Talking of Finance, a note was included in the Monthly Letter urging WIs to consider the Financial Campaign for the Defence of the Country (National Savings Scheme) which was being launched by the National Savings Association, suggesting consideration should also be given to speakers on the subject.

Food and petrol rationing had by now come into force and therefore county meetings were very much curtailed. Bulk petrol coupons had been received by the County and would only be supplied through the County Secretary. Drama suggested WIs might like to work up a Variety Entertainment during the winter months. This might consist of short plays, recitations, dancing, percussion band, etc. Music suggested small choirs should be formed and meet in private houses – singing parties to be organised by the committee for those WIs applying for them.

Organisation wished to hold a Conveners' Conference and Mrs. Nugent Harris was to be asked to speak on Group work in wartime.

Agriculture and Horticulture with the Produce Guild suggested Area Depots be set up for the preserving of fruit, according to the Agriculture and Fisheries Scheme, possibly in each Group; two canning machines should be bought at £7.10s. each; Miss Webster should remain secretary of the Produce Guild and make all arrangements for conferences and schools in conjunction with the office. Three meetings were organised – at Moulton which 102 attended, at Deene Park with 150 present and at Thorpe Mandeville with 104. Demonstrations were arranged at these meetings on Vegetable Cookery, Drying Vegetables, Storing Vegetables, Fruit Bottling, Trussing and Dressing Poultry.

A request had been received for members to correspond with

Ministry of Food Ration Book.

American members and this was to be put in the Monthly letter, and details of speakers on the subject of vaccination should be sent to WIs as this appeared to be a very urgent question.

A scheme whereby Fruit Trees were to be sold to WIs had been drawn up and this would be relayed to them via the Monthly Letter. Orders had already been placed for 3,378 Raspberry bushes, 1,409 Blackcurrant, 378 Redcurrant and 726 Gooseberry. In addition £186 of Onion (600 packets) and Tomato seeds (100) had been ordered.

At about this time sugar was being supplied by the Ministry of Food for the preservation of surplus fruit in the form of jam-making and

Mrs. Dickens (nee Webster) was appointed 'Sugar Secretary' with expenses of £10 for her work.

Organisation were suggesting four programme planning meetings with Miss Christmas as the Speaker. At this time she was a member of National's team, later going to Denman.. The Annual Meeting on 11th December 1940 attracted 200 members, 72 of whom were delegates each collecting Pooling of Fares of 2/11d. Executive members were re-appointed and this is when Mrs. Macdonald- Buchanan of Cottesbrooke joined their number. Sub-committees were re-appointed en bloc and Handicrafts were quick to suggest that a Handicraft Thrift competition should be arranged at one monthly meeting during the year, hoping that later in the Autumn these would be followed up by a small Thrift Exhibition; the Produce Guild asked for four classes for Produce to be incorporated in this.

Label used in fruit canning.

Organisation wished to postpone until the Autumn the drive for new WIs, as they were all very busy in the villages during May with the Preservation Centres; National had offered Miss Christmas as the speaker.

The emphasis at this time was mainly on the Fruit Preservation Centres, and it is from these undoubtedly that the WI has gained its reputation as being jam-makers. To quote Mrs. Dickens 'nowadays folk rather smile about the WI Jam image but thanks to those early members who took advice generously given the standard rose and WI excellence has proved itself'. 127 Centres were registered in Northamptonshire, and although it was hard work it was very worthwhile.

Many old coppers came into their own but often the owners looked askance at using their fuel to make them boil, so all the members brought some of their own ration. Jam Schools were held and the Board of Education offered to run these and provide instructors. Packets of seeds had been received from America and these were to be ballotted for amongst WIs having Produce Guild members. America had also sent supplies of Super Phosphate and Derris Powder, and

Northamptonshire applied for a share of this. A special Jam School was organised at Peterborough taken by Mrs. Dickens, Miss Law, the Assistant Secretary and Mrs. Dodson (Executive). Mrs. Dickens had war-time recipes for home-grown forced rhubarb, unusual ways of using Brussels sprouts and many others issued by the Ministry of Food. Members were urged 'to turn on your wireless at 8.15 every morning for useful tips and recipes'. Mrs. Dickens also helped with the Country Pie scheme in villages where there was no British Restaurant to help out by providing food.

Here we were in 1941, too, talking about Post War arrangements – or perhaps it was just the nature of the WI to be thinking ahead and planning for the future. Whatever, four Post War Planning Conferences were scheduled at Northampton, Polebrooke, Kettering and Helmdon, one of the speakers again being Miss Christmas and the other Mrs. Gowring, both of National. WI Programmes and Speakers and Demonstrators were the subjects of some of the discussions, and various competitions were to be held . This year saw the subscription raised to 2/6d. with 5d. going to National 7d. to County and 1/6d. remaining with WIs. This was the first time it had been increased since being set at 2s., one tenth of an agricultural worker's wage in 1916. Up to August 1941, 10,000 lbs of jam had been made; this had all been helped by the Ministry of Food supplying sugar and also contributing towards funds. The Ministry of Supply helped by releasing supplies of cans and jars quickly. Arrangements were made to sell the produce on market stalls all over the country, charging the same price as grocers. Supplies of fruit were paid for at market rates. Although a special sugar ration for making fruit into jam was not available in the early stages it became available later to make plum, greengage and damson jam.

10,000 Dixie Hand Sealers (home canners) came from America where nearly every woman had a home canning machine. It was the size of a large mincer and clamped on the table in the same way. They came with a complete Food Preservation Unit and Oil Stoves, preserving pans, tea towels, thermometers, bottling jars, jam pot covers and special discs for pickles and chutneys. The Centres only dealt with fruit which could not be used by the grower or transported to a factory and therefore would go to waste. After rationing started in 1941, the scheme came under the Ministry of Food. Members sold their fruit to the centres for a fixed government price, but members worked voluntarily in the centres. They were not allowed to buy anything themselves. All jam and cans were collected and taken to central

Marketing new style – Customer; Miss Law, Assistant Secretary; Seller Hon. Mrs. Macdonald-Buchanan.

wholesale depots.

Mrs. Dickens had sent a letter of thanks for her wedding present, so she was obviously married in early 1941. Her husband served with the Royal Air Force. The March 1941 meeting of Executive suggested Agriculture and Horticulture should consider starting a Market Stall in Northampton. Finances were still proving a problem so agreed the Quota for 1942 should be increased by 3d. to 1/4d. per member. Mrs. Macdonald-Buchanan offered to hold a Party at Cottesbrooke in the summer and this was accepted. Miss Law, the Assistant Secretary, was to be paid £2 per hour and become more of a full time assistant.

The Produce Guild was to hold 24 meetings in the year, 12 in the North and 12 in the South; if possible 6 centres to hold two meetings each. There would be additional meetings every two months at Moulton, Mr. Middleton to be asked to speak at two/three meetings. This is the gardening Mr. Middleton of radio fame, who was in fact the son of the gardener at the home of Mrs.Sacheverell Sitwell at Weston Hall – she had been elected to Executive in 1940. A conference on

Agricultural Work was to be held in May by the Produce Guild and 10,000 cans were to be stored – 5,000 each by Mrs. Macdonald Buchanan and Mrs. Dickens.

Miss Joan Wake had asked for a WI competition for old photographs of people taken before 1914. An exhibition would be held and Lord Berners would be asked to open. This did eventually take place in November 1943 and 60 people attended the opening, the exhibition lasting for a fortnight.

Northamptonshire sent a protest to National stating that the AGM should not be held in London in June 1942 as it was unpatriotic in wartime conditions with difficulties of transport when petrol should be saved.

The Annual Meeting in March 1942 was held at the Angel Hotel. Prizes were awarded for two Essay competitions – for the Ideal Home essay Yelvertoft was

Hon. Mrs. Macdonald-Buchanan, Chairman, Produce Guild.

awarded the first prize with Long Buckby second and for the Educational essay Long Buckby received first prize with Boughton second. The results of the Mending competition were also announced, 47 entries having been received: Darning – Brackley with full marks, Patching Hackleton. The speaker talked about China and the part women were taking in the war there. There was no election for Executive at this meeting as Mrs. Lester Reid, Thorpe Mandeville, and Mrs. Cunnington, Long Buckby, had been nominated making 16 nominations for 15 places.

The promised Cottesbrooke Garden Party was held on 25th June

Collecting salvage. Gt. Billing, 1943.

and, in addition to Mr. Middleton speaking here, a Brains Trust answered questions, and there was a Bring and Buy; also stalls illustrating the work of the Produce Guild. Charges for the day were 2s. for reserved seats and 1s. for unreserved. Tea was 1s. and the Garden Party was open to all. Proceeds were £68 10s. This was followed by a similar Party at Thorpe Mandeville on 25th August.

A copy of 'Good Programmes for Hard Times' to be sent to all WIs, cost 24s. Into 1943, and the sad news at the beginning of the year was that Miss Mary Bouverie had died at Delapre Abbey which had been the home of the Bouverie family since 1756 when it was let by them to John Cooper, Northampton boot and shoe manufacturer in 1905. Miss Bouverie had moved back to the Abbey in 1914 and that was when we heard of so many WI events being held in the grounds of Delapre which were considerable with about 500 acres of parkland and 8 acres of more formal gardens. The War Office took over the Abbey in 1940 and Miss Bouverie moved to Duston, later returning to rooms over the stables in 1942. In 1946 Northampton Corporation purchased the estate for £56,000 and the War Office eventually gave up the use of the Abbey in 1948. By a strange quirk of fate the Abbey later housed the Northamptonshire Record Office, of which Miss Joan Wake was the

Archivist. She, too, you will remember had been a member of Executive and was responsible for the writing of so many WI Village histories following her instructive booklet on How to compile a Village History.

In February 1943 a Preservation Display was staged at the Dig for Victory Campaign event. At the beginning of 1943 Britain needed more and more food as the U-Boat Campaign hit hard. By the end of the year the country was less dependent on overseas supplies as the work done by the Women's Land Army was sufficient to keep Britain in food. Although food rationing continued after the war, the Women's Land Army continued until 1950 when it was disbanded. The Annual Meeting was held in March at the Town Hall when the morning speaker was Arthur Bryant on Local Government. The Pooling of Fares was 2/8d. The afternoon session was in the form of an Exhibition.

Work continued apace at the Preservation Centres. Jam Schools were held at Banbury, Northampton, Oundle and Peterborough. Tomato meetings were held at Long Buckby, Boddington, Old Stratford and Moulton with cultivation, cookery and preservation all being covered. Mrs. Macdonald-Buchanan had started two market stalls at Creaton and Brixworth and kindly offered help to any other WIs wishing to do the same.

Carol Concerts were held at Earls Barton and Flore and throughout

Household Jobbery School – Fixing a new washer.

> NATIONAL FEDERATION OF WOMEN'S INSTITUTES
>
> Registered No. 22
>
> MINISTRY of FOOD SCHEME for FRUIT PRESERVATION
>
> The Ministry of Food has approved the issue by the N.F.W.I. of a CERTIFICATE OF COMPETENCE to members qualified to be in charge of a canning machine at a Co-operative Preservation Centre
>
> *This is to Certify that*
>
> Mrs. Dickens,
>
> Address 1 Talbot Road, Northampton.
>
> of the Northamptonshire County Federation is hereby declared qualified to take charge of Canning at a Co-operative Preservation Centre under the above scheme
>
> Signed *D.J. Yn Kinson*
> Chairman, N.F.W.I. Agriculture Sub-committee
>
> Countersigned *Elizabeth HKO*
> N.F.W.I. Agricultural Secretary,
> Date of issue 22nd January, 1944.   39 Eccleston Street, London, S.W.1

Ministry of Food Certificate for Fruit Preservation.

the county in various halls and churches. A Music Festival was held at Spratton, with £6.4.0d. being taken. Miss Ciceley McCall had written a book ' Women's Institutes' a copy of which had been sent to all WIs by the publishers, again at a cost of 24s.

A Cottesbrooke Rally was to be organised and more Jam Schools were to be held, four members of the committee had been appointed canning demonstrators by National, and on 18th March 1944 a Market Stall was opened in Northampon.

Miss Agnes Stops of Duston had obviously returned from New Zealand by this time as she was being asked to attend a VCO Refresher School in September. I think it is appropriate here to talk a little more about Miss Stops as she was also one of the pioneers of the WI and was a keen and enthusiastic VCO. On reading her fascinating diaries one can always detect the same keen spirit which has, during such a long and useful lifetime, prompted her to work for the development of

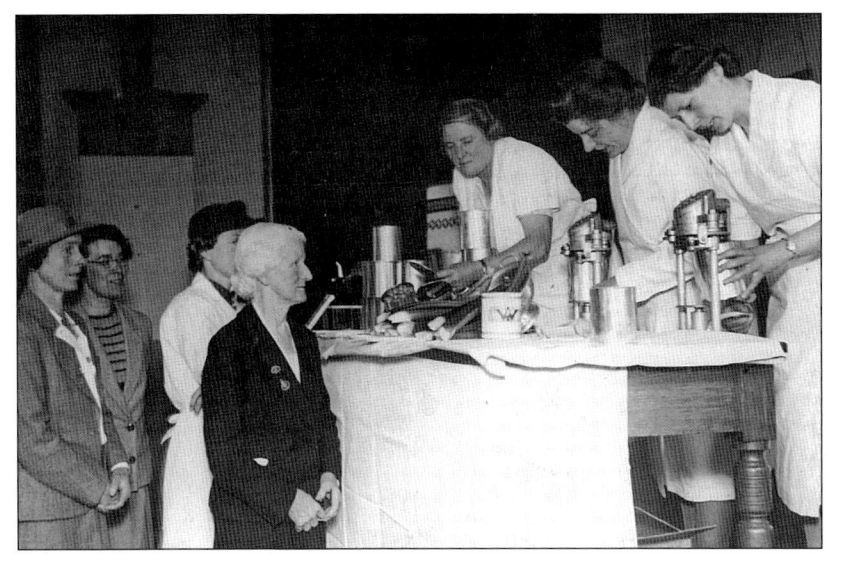

*One Day Canning School, 1944 – Mrs. Downing (Executive), Mrs. Dickens (Secretary Produce Guild), Miss Law (Assistant Secretary).
In Front: Mrs. Barker (County Secretary).*

women's lives in many parts of the world. In addition to her county commitments she spent many months in New Zealand and the South Sea Islands as Organiser forming over 200 WIs, and learning much of their crafts, some of which she mastered and demonstrated to institutes at home. During the next decade Miss Stops travelled extensively in Australia, where her exciting experiences included speaking at a meeting in the Great Hall in Melbourne which held 10,000 people. Her talk was broadcast on the ABC World Network. From Australia she travelled to South Africa where she became friends with many famous people such as General and Mrs. Smuts.

Miss Stops was several times a member of the British Delegation which attended meetings of the International Council of Women, in Sweden and Edinburgh, and whilst attending the latter was asked by the BBC to give the English Visitor's Talk. During the early years of World War II she again spent several months in Australia and South Africa.

Reported in October that Mrs. Barker was ill and Miss Law was to act as Secretary in her absence.

A Christmas Sale in November raised £80 and plans were well in

Kislingbury – Drama, 1945.

hand for the Competition for Cottages for Rural Workers. The schedule for this was for the best plan by an RDC Architect for a pair of rural cottages and was very detailed. In 1944 a booklet was printed showing the winning designs. Mock-ups were made for exhibition purposes and eventually the winning designs were erected at various sites, one being Cottesbrooke. Models of the winning designs were made and taken to venues throughout the County and nationally.

A letter had been received from the Director of Education stating the Government wished the provision of school meals to be stepped up to about 75% of the population. WIs were thanked for their help, both voluntary and paid, either through the WVS or individually. Paid members cooked the meals in village centres and these were distributed by volunteers.

In August Miss Joan Wake asked if WI 1943 programmes could be collected so that the Record Society could house these as a matter of interest for future generations.

The year finished with a Produce Guild Secretaries' meeting at Moulton, followed by a Pig Curing course. It was recommended at this time that the Produce Guild Secretary, Mrs. M. Dickens should have an honorarium of £45, following a report that 8,166 lbs of jam had been made in the county, and Executive were very appreciative of the work she had done.

The Annual Meeting on 22nd March 1944 was attended by over 200 visitors, 98 of whom were delegates. The speaker was Miss Tompkinson, National Agricultural Adviser.

Three or four events took place in April, firstly the Long Buckby Music Festival. This was most successful with the conductor being Miss Singleton, County Music Adviser. The Produce Guild organised a visit to a Flax Mill for members, Organisation arranged a Secretaries/Treasurers Conference at which Miss Chamberlain of National spoke.

Handicrafts arranged classes on Rushwork but felt these had not been well supported although 57 had attended at Northampton, 54 at Peterborough and 54 at Banbury, all venues bearing in mind the ease of getting there by public transport A Conference on the Constitution was held at Leamington Spa for Warwickshire and neighbouring counties, including Northamptonshire.

Chapter 6
TAKING TIME TO RECOVER
1945–1960

A message from HM the Queen to her Fellow WI Members was printed in Home & Country stating she 'knew what difficulties the WI have had to overcome in meeting wartime conditions. Members have done much important National Service, including work for evacuees, co-operative work on comforts for Men of the Services, and Hospital supplies; also co-operative buying of vegetable and potato seeds to increase our food supply. I congratulate you with all my heart on this good work. I hear that monthly meetings have been held often under great difficulties and that they have maintained their high level and have proved more than ever a welcome source of strength and refreshment to members and visitors. Knowing, as I do, the great value of the WI to the life of the community, I send my good wishes, and rejoice in the sure knowledge that, whatever they may be asked to do, my fellow members will not fail.'

Everyone must have been feeling by January 1945 that the war would seen be over, but some months were to pass before this actually happened.

January found the new Executive meeting with Miss Stops and Mrs. Dickens joining their number. Sadly Mrs. Wentworth Watson was resigning. A new sub-committee **MARKETING** was suggested and members were appointed under the chairmanship of Mrs. Macdonald Buchanan. It was reported at this time that the Northampton Market stall had been open for one year and it was doing so well that consideration was being given to opening another.

A Drama Adviser was also appointed and a one-day school for Drama Producers was held in Northampton. It was also reported that 4,020 letters in all had been sent out, 911 Produce Guild letters, 910 Preservation Centre letters, 44 parcels of seeds and 168 letters about Market Stalls and the rest general correspondence.

Music Festivals were held at Wellingborough in February with 144 adult singers and 100 children; with a second one in Oundle at Easter.

There was much talk about a new constitution but finally National decided to defer any such changes until more normal conditions prevailed and until more younger members were able to take part.

The Annual Meeting was held in the Town Hall, Northampton on 29th March when the speaker had been Miss Mary Day of the Home Section of the Farmers' Weekly speaking on Rural Housing. The Federation's Model Houses were on view and the Housing booklets were also on sale. It was decided these Houses could be hired out for a small fee, but that they would have to be insured for a cost of £1.1.0d. per year. 200 members had attended, 84 of whom were delegates and the pooling of fares was 3/4d. The meeting ended with Choirs singing some of their Festival music and the whole meeting joining in community singing.

Just to show there is nothing really new, when I was again Chairman of Membership in 2003/4, we held area meetings when we demonstrated how WI business should not be done followed by our suggestions as to how it should be conducted. Well, two conferences were held in Banbury and Northampton in 1945 covering exactly the same theme. I rather imagine they were two very different interpretations with a gap of 60 years occurring between the two!

In May we saw the end of the war in Europe with VE Day.

Reported the Chief Constable would be attending the June meeting of Executive to discuss the possibility of him speaking to WIs on Road Safety.

In June also the National Federation held probably the most momentus meeting of its existence when the membership gave its approval through a resolution proposed by Oxfordshire that the National Executive should buy, equip and open a College for WI members. Much discussion had taken place before reaching this stage but more of this later.

Victory in Japan came in August and so World War II ended. However, rationing was still in place and continued to be so until 1953.

Northamptonshire's year of 1945 finished with a Christmas Sale on 29th November in the Gas Showrooms in the afternoon, which raised £80 for Produce Guild funds.

1946 was the year Lady Denman retired and she was succeeded by Lady Albemarle. Work also started on a large wall hanging size 15'3 x 9' to be called 'The Work of Women in Wartime'. It started life in Winchester when a representative from each county was taught the stitches to be used, which they in turn taught to their own county members. Our representative was Miss Clare of Towcester, and the six other selected members to work on this tapestry were Mrs. Hobson,

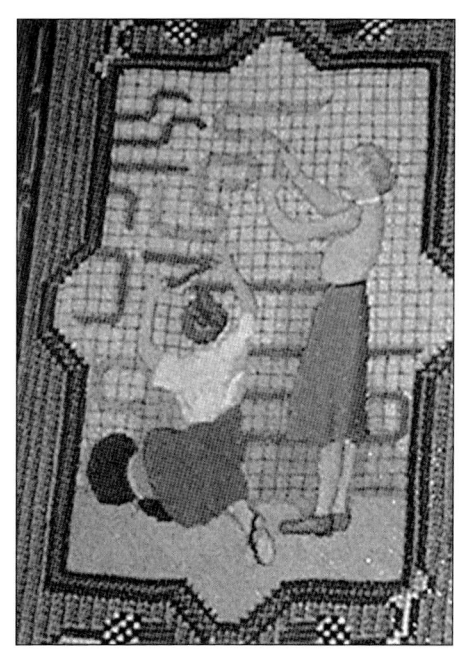

The 'Work of Women in Wartime' Wallhanging made by WI members.

Wappenham, Mrs. Millar, Blisworth, Mrs. Kirk, Overstone, Mrs. Downing, Old Stratford and Miss Law, Billing. Eventually 400 members were involved in this effort and it was originally displayed in the Victoria and Albert Museum when a National Craft Exhibition was held there. The tapestry was worked in wool with panels showing various aspects of women's war time work, joined with scrolls and borders. I believe it is now in the Imperial War Museum.

In 1946 Miss Law, the County Secretary resigned and Miss Berridge was appointed, the first grant was applied for from the LEA and £250 was allocated to the WI. A WI market was opened at Badby. There was only one Council Meeting this year but 110 delegates attended as well as over 100 other visitors; and there were 5418 members at this time. The afternoon session consisted of an entertainment by members of the Music and Drama sub-committee produced by Mrs. Bailey of Ravensthorpe.

The March 1947 Annual Meeting was proclaimed the best attended for some years with 112 delegates and well over 200 visitors. Mr. Kenneth MacWhirter, secretary of the Rural Community Council spoke on the newly formed Councils and Mrs. Spencer Smith, member of National Executive spoke on the varied International Work of the National Federation. An urgency resolution asked for those WI members in isolated areas to request their Parish Councils to accumulate a village coal dump during the summer months for use in an emergency. The entertainment included a short scene from Henry V and two verse speaking items from members of Blisworth.

To take up this drama theme, after the war from 1947 to 1949 festivals were held at Watford Court, the home of Lady Henley who was still Chairman of the Drama committee. The interest in drama increased at this time and the festivals moved to the Exeter Hall, Northampton, where they continued until 1959. It would seem that members still had time to devote to outside interests such as drama and this outlet was probably much needed after the depressing war years. There were large numbers of entries and there were packed houses from Monday to Friday, with Saturday being 'the day'. Tickets were in great demand and had to be purchased well in advance. The programme for these days was usually performances of three plays followed by tea served by waitresses of the Co-op in their neat black dresses and white caps and aprons – all for the price of 2s. This was followed by the judging and summing up by the adjudicators who were very well-known actors of that time.

The Half-Yearly Council Meeting, held at Wicksteed Park, Kettering on 8th October was attended by 234 members, 100 of whom were delegates. Delegates always sat in the front of the hall, and the pooling of fares was 3s. at this meeting. In the morning, Mrs. Watson, the honorary secretary of the Elizabeth Fry Centenary Fund explained this scheme to provide training for women who had neglected their homes and children, resulting in their being given a prison sentence. An experimental home had been set up at Farnham for a period of five years and funds were needed for this project.

The afternoon session consisted of a Parade of Period Costumes, Resolutions and Community Singing. Mrs. Bailey of Ravensthorpe produced the Parade and caused much enjoyment with seven examples of different periods, some dresses being lent and worn by their owners, those being admired most were two from Benefield which were particularly lovely.

1948 began to see things returning to normal, although the lives of women in the community had changed for ever. There was no doubt WI membership did decrease during the war years, reaching a low of 288,000 in 1943. However, it was left to individuals to decide for themselves how they could best serve their country in wartime. Many members were called into active service. Those who remained found many avenues for helping the war effort, much of this being done through the WIs themselves.

Northamptonshire was visited on 24th March 1948 by the honorary treasurer of National, Mrs. Methuen JB who talked about the proposed raising of the subscription which would be brought before the next National AGM She quoted figures illustrating the enormous increase in administrative costs and overhead expenses. The discussion on the subscription did in fact take place at the National AGM and this time the new subscription was 3/6d., 1s. going to National (an increase of 7d.), 1/6d to Counties (an increase of 11d.) and 1s., remaining with WIs. After this talk and the resolutions, two one-act plays were performed, *OHMS* by Earls Barton and *Check to the Queen* by Brackley. Drama certificates were presented with Brackley winning the Drama Cup.

Princess Elizabeth was married in April this year and the Federation sent her a wedding present, and there was yet another reprint of the Cookery Book. This time the cost was £100 for 2,000 copies, and they were sold for 2s. each. We were recently contacted by a bookseller in Hay on Wye who had acquired a copy of this edition wondering whether we wished to purchase it! The Duchess of Gloucester attended a Pageant of Women of Northamptonshire from 1200 to 1948 held at Delapre. With fact and fancy the Pageant ran through the years to an epilogue in a 1948 War Mime. Supporting the Pageant were displays of handicrafts with demonstrations in lace, spinning and weaving, toy making, glove making and slipper making. There were also samples of jam and canned and bottled fruit and vegetables. The gardeners from Cottesbrooke arranged a general horticultural display, as did the head gardener from St. Andrew's Hospital. There were several interesting trade exhibits and experts from the Ministry of Food gave demonstrations in cooking.

Now we come back to that momentous occasion when all eyes were focussed on the WI's new venture, our own adult education college I have mentioned the resolution at the 1945 National AGM, following which there were two groups who were instrumental in pushing forward with this idea. There was a nucleus of members of National Executive who were enthusiastic and also some Oxfordshire Federation members, mainly Miss Helena Deneke and Mrs. Elizabeth Brunner, the latter having in fact been elected to National Executive in 1943.

The early history of residential colleges developed from the Folk High Schools in Denmark. Sir Richard Livingstone a double first scholar from Oxford who became President of Corpus Christi believed education should continue throughout life; children at that time ceased their education at either 13 or 14. He was delivering a lecture on 'Education in a World Adrift' at Radbrook Domestic Science College in Shrewsbury which was attended by two members of National staff, Miss Elizabeth Christmas, the General Organiser, and Miss Cecily McCall, Education sub-committee organiser, both of whom had made education their concern. In his lecture he deplored the fact that in the Government White Paper of the day there was no provision for adult education and then posed the question 'Why don't the Women's Institutes fill the gap? Why not start a college of your own?' This was the beginning of the idea of a College and due to the continued efforts of Sir Richard and the National Federation the decision was taken in 1945 to go ahead with this idea.

Many houses were visited but it was not until November 1945 that Marcham Park was found. It had come on the market having been de-requisitioned from the Air Ministry and was a late Georgian mansion in a hundred acres of parkland. There was a lake and two cottages, with a large walled garden.

Northamptonshire has a connection with Denman in that the owner of Marcham Park from 1789–1810 was George Elwes and he had married Amelia Alt of Northamptonshire (Billing Hall was the home of the Elwes family until its demolition in 1956), It was their daughter Emily Duffield, who rebuilt Denman as we know it to-day in 1820, and her picture still hangs in the house. The house remained in the Duffield family until 1938 when it was bought by Mr. Berners who modernised it but never lived in it, because at the beginning of the war it was requisitioned by the Air Ministry. National signed the contract in December 1945 to purchase for £16,000. In the end it was decided £60,000 was needed to purchase it and equip the College and funding was the next major concern. The Carnegie Trust who had helped the

Denman College.

WI in the past, both with rural industries in 1918 and for training drama producers and choir conductors, and providing a National organiser for WI markets in later years, was approached. They kindly gave a grant of £20,000 and the remainder was to be raised by the WIs themselves. National Chairman, Lady Albemarle, wrote to every WI reminding them of the 1945 mandate and inviting each of them to raise £10 over three years. By the end of 1946 £4,000 had been received and promises of a further £27,000 had been given. By 1947 £40,000 had been raised. The Appeal was eventually closed in 1953 when £66,000 had been raised.

Lady Brunner was Chairman of the College committee during this time and was responsible for the re-furbishment. County Federations undertook to provide the soft furnishing for the bedrooms. Coupons were provided by one county so that household linen could be bought – because we still had rationing – crockery was provided by another. In fact, as is usual with WIs, everything that was needed for the College was provided by one or other County or Company. By January 1948 some of the committee picknicked in the empty house sitting on packing cases round a log fire. By the end of April house and garden were pronounced fit to receive visitors and that summer 640 delegates to the London AGM in London were brought by coaches to see their college for the first time. In fact, before the official opening more than 7,000 members had already visited the College. At that time it could only house 30 students. Because of complications with building licences, rationing and shortage of materials it was not possible to extend, and it was only thanks to the kindness and generosity of Counties, WIs, and individual friends from all over the country that the College was ready for opening. On 1st September the resident staff moved in and on 24th September Sir Richard Livingstone cut the ribbon for the official opening in the presence of Lady Denman, Lady Albemarle and Lady Brunner, as well as representatives from all the County Federations of England and Wales. For Northamptonshire Mrs. Tynan, a member of Executive from Isham, attended.

When it came to deciding on a name for the College, at the first AGM after the war in 1946 when the Queen attended, a happy solution was found when Lady Denman announced she had decided not to stand again for chairmanship. She had served for 30 years, and on taking the chair Lady Albemarle took over and suggested the name of Denman for the College as a memorial to Lady Denman, to which she is said to have replied 'I think that is a lovely idea'.

The first Warden of Denman was Miss Elizabeth Christmas who had

Opening Day – Lady Albemarle and Lady Brunner with Sir Richard Livingstone and Miss Christmas (warden).

done so much towards getting a WI college established. She had a warm and vivid personality and worked devotedly for Denman until she died in 1956. Her successor was the other National member who had helped with the initial proposal for a College, Miss Cecily McCall who remained in office until 1959.

With Denman going ahead with its plans we can now go back to Northamptonshire – how lucky we all are to live in a county so near the College – and look at the Half-Yearly Council Meeting which was held at Wicksteed Park, Kettering on 13th October. 232 members attended, 78 of whom were delegates. In the morning the Garden & Allotment Certificates and Cups were presented and the speaker was Dr. Gray Turner talking on the National Health Service. This was the year we were to see the start of the NHS, following the Beveridge Report, with all it benefits. Discussions followed in the afternoon on venues of future Council meetings and it was suggested that these should be at Oundle and Towcester, but the Brackley delegate stated it was not possible for them to get to Oundle. Another discussion gave the members the opportunity to pay for a printed newsletter but this was rejected. The day ended with entertainment provided by Cogenhoe, Ravensthorpe and Flore WIs.

1949 saw the Hon. Mrs. Macdonald Buchanan take over the chair from Mrs. Renton of Guilsborough who had held this post for 10 years. At her first Council Meeting, which was held in the Town Hall, Northampton, on 23rd March 138 delegates attended with over 170 visitors. For the first time we see the balance sheet go over £1,000, and the pooling of fares were down to 2/11d. Mrs. John Bell was the speaker on the Food Question and the Country Women of the World. It was at this meeting there was a resolution urging bakers to wrap their bread. A very long and varied programme of entertainment took place in the afternoon, first of all with six choirs singing their own choices then Lt. Houghton producing *Sanctuary*. There followed a musical Trio in D Minor from Mendelssohn's first movement, finishing with *The Six Wives of Calais* performed by Flore WI. The programme for this entertainment cost 3d.

In memory of Mrs. Agnes Watt, who had died in the Autumn of 1948, 300 lime trees were planted at Denman College to provide an avenue leading into one of the College entrances, these being funded by asking each WI to donate £1, some institutes combining to provide this gift. The Half-Yearly Council Meeting was held in the Town Hall, Towcester, on 14th October and 200 members attended including 80 delegates. The speaker was Mr. Charles Lines on The National Trust and he was able to use lantern slides in this hall. The lantern was a portable film lantern which contained an electric battery. The special advantages were 1) it required no skill in working and any member could turn the handle for the lecturer; 2) any lecturer could get pictures, photos, postcards, etc. made into a film for the extremely reasonable price of 3d. each. The pictures were very clear, even in an imperfectly darkened room These film lanterns were used in WIs and had often be hired and sent by rail. Most WIs would probably have a station nearby from which the lantern could be collected, and they were used from the thirties onwards because very few villages had an electricity supply.

There had been 38 entries for the Gardens and Allotments Competition and the awards were presented after resolutions had been taken. Also the prizewinner of the ACWW Essay competition was acknowledged. The afternoon was taken up with a short talk on analgesia i.e. the use of gas and air in childbirth given by Miss Williams the Nursing Officer for Northamptonshire, and also talks from a county midwife and a mother who had had experience of the machine. The meeting ended with a performance by the Percussion Band and a one-act play, *The Princess and the Woodcutter*.

In 1950 Cogenhoe's social half hour was broadcast on the BBC and a record was made of this which WIs could buy; also a photographic competition was launched for pictures which could be used to made a County Calendar.

The Annual Council Meeting in the Town Hall, Northampton on 15th March was attended by the National Chairman, Lady Albemarle, together with 141 delegates and a further 190 visitors. Lady Albemarle spoke of the importance of living peaceably together in villages; otherwise what hope was there for an international peace. She also mentioned the many ways open to members for broadening their interests and urged them to be ready to accept responsibilities.

The day ended with an entertainment consisting of songs by WI choirs and a Mime Play called *Priscilla*. All the costumes were made by members, having been designed by Mrs. Jones of West Haddon.

October saw the County Executive honouring its commitment to move the Half-Yearly Council meeting around the county in that it was held at the Victoria Hall in Oundle on 4th October. 164 members managed to attend, including delegates from 78 WIs.

Discussions were held on many subjects including the disbanding of the Produce Guild, Mrs. Dickens explaining that although members would still be entitled to take Canning tests they would not be eligible to take any of the Produce Guild Tests. Members were asked to take this matter back to their WIs for further consideration.

The next subject was on mobile dispensaries, Lowick describing instances of hardship where journeys had to be made in order to have a prescription made up; regulations stipulated that these could only be handled on registered premises.

Housing of old people was next on the agenda and reference was made to a scheme whereby old people might be cared for under conditions which did not resemble those of an Institution. One suggestion was that small houses in villages could be used. Home Helps was another suggestion, implying that WI members might render valuable service in their own villages by offering to relieve those who had old people to look after.

One other subject was taken, that an Annual Report listing the names and addresses of WI officers in the county should be published but it was to be 1957 before a published Year Book was printed giving the information required.

The wife of the American Naval Attache spoke on some striking comparisons of the ways in which the life of the American countrywoman differed from our own, and then a senior member of the Upper House of the Ceylon Parliament was introduced. She conveyed greetings from the WIs in Ceylon where the movement had played such a large part in raising the standard of living, particularly with regard to the health services.

The meeting concluded with entertainment in the form of songs from Vaughan Williams' Cantata for women's voices performed by Oundle, followed by a mime. The Cantata had been the original concept of Miss Nancy Tennant, the National Vice-Chairman who took over from Miss Grace Hadow. She was an accomplished musician and conductor and was appointed Music Adviser to National. This was an honorary post, but she travelled throughout the country adjudicating at county Music Festivals, including Northamptonshire. For nearly a year. 1,230 choirs, comprising 21,000 members practised Folk Songs of the Four Seasons. The final concert was performed at the Royal Albert Hall when the massed choirs were accompanied by the London Symphony Orchestra conducted by Sir Adrian Boult. The British Council, which had given financial support, reported that it was one of the outstanding events of the year in amateur music making.

In 1951 Mrs. Lankester, East Haddon. succeeded Mrs. Macdonald-Buchanan as County Chairman and Mrs.Clarke was co-opted to take on the role of Honorary Treasurer. Countess Spencer was still President and she chaired the Annual Council Meeting held in the Town Hall, Northampton on 4th April, when 137 delegates attended in addition to 190 visitors. Drama certificates were presented to the successful performers in the Festival held the previous November and two short talks were given by members who had attended courses at Denman College – Mrs. Clarke of Evenley and Mrs. Mordaunt of Castle Ashby. The speaker on this occasion was Dr. J. Grant, Director of the Oxford Regional Blood Transfusion Service and he gave details of the benefits which were derived in both medicine and surgery from those who volunteered to act as blood donors. The day ended with entertainment organised by Music and Drama sub-committee members, which included a performance of the winning play in the Novice Class at the Drama Festival – *The Jilted Pair* by Cold Ashby and Thornby.

The County Federations involved in the East of England Show were greatly honoured by the visit of HRH Princess Elizabeth to the Exhibit jointly staged by Northants and Hunts and Peterborough. She was accompanied by HRH The Duchess of Gloucester and showed much interest in the handicraft and agricultural exhibits. She graciously accepted lace edged handkerchiefs which Mrs. Millar, Blisworth. had made.

A Spring Produce Show was held when over 800 entries were received; Stowe IX Churches won the Cup. The cake classes and the floral decoration classes received good entries and were a source of delight to the many visitors. This was a two-day show and a display of crafts was staged here also. A record of nearly 1,000 handicraft entries were received. A wide range of crafts were exhibited in the WI tent at the County Show at Overstone later in the year, as well as a display of musical instruments.

Seven Area Agricultural meetings were held, and also two Moulton Days. Among the subjects demonstrated were Horticulture, Cookery, Flower Wiring, Floral Decoration and the new Deep Freeze method of preserving. Canning Schools were still being held, and a two-day Bacon Curing School was most successful being attended by 35 members who enjoyed practical work under the helpful instruction of Miss Swingler, Rural Domestic Economy Instructress at Moulton.

Prunella, the play by Lawrence Housman and H. Granville Barker, was performed firstly at the New Theatre, then in the open air in gardens at Barnwell, Thorpe Mandeville and Brockhall. At each of the garden performances a display of The Life and Death of the Gooseberry was arranged when all the stages of the gooseberry, from cuttings to the preserving of the fruit were demonstrated. A display of crafts was also staged at these performances.

Members took part in two very popular outings, the first to the Billing Flax Mills and the second to Bugbrooke Flour Mills.

Turnover for the Northampton Market had increased and had reached just over £1,000 with nearly £900 being paid back to the producers.

A record entry of 29 plays was received for the Drama Festival. The Cup was won by Castle Ashby with Flore as runners-up, and the Novice Shield by Weekly and Warkton with Milton Malsor second.

The event of the year was of course the Festival of Britain on the South Bank. The Official Opening Ceremony by HM King George VI took place at St. Paul's Cathedral on 3rd May. One offshoot of this was the Country Wife Mural designed by Constance Howard, Principal of the London Art School. This depicts various WI activities and many

The Country Wife Mural designed by Constance Howard for Festival of Britain 1951 and presented to NFWI.

members made samples of tiny gloves, slippers, baskets, etc. which were appliquéd on. This was eventually presented to the NFWI and is now kept in the lecture room at Denman College. Its major claim to fame is that Mary Quant, who was a student at the School, was responsible for making the pink blouse in the centre of the mural.

The County Council grant remained at £250 which enabled the county to meet all expenses; we now had a turnover of £2,830 with a membership of 8,110. Noted that a county Denman Bursary was just £2.10.0d.

At the Half-Yearly Council meeting on 3rd October at Wicksteed Park, Kettering, discussions took place on the question of WIs supporting outside charities and whether future Produce and Handicraft Exhibitions should be held at the same time. It was stressed that the support and work of the WI should have prior claim on time and energy with regard to fund raising, and it was thought the two Exhibitions should be combined.

Mrs. Hardwick of the Hunts Federation, and also a member of National *Home and Country* gave latest facts and figures to illustrate the growth and development of the magazine.

Lady Tweedsmuir spoke on The Pleasures of Reading and Writing which members found most helpful as well as amusing.

Finally a parade of costumes from 1851 to 1951 was arranged. Many original costumes were worn illustrating the changes in fashion over the last century.

The Denman Cup, which is now awarded annually for a piece of creative writing with the subject being decided by National, was originally offered at the Dairy Show in 1951. This first year it was open

The Festival of Britain Catalogue Cover, 1951

Twenty-first Birthday Celebration, Isham 1951. Mrs. Lankester (left) and Mrs. Tynan.

to the best co-operative exhibit 1 bottle fruit, 1 bottle solid pack apples or pears in syrup, 1 bottle solid pack tomatoes, 1 lb. jar blackcurrant jam, 1 lb. jar raspberry jam, half a pound of any variety red or light coloured jelly, 1 10 oz. jar green tomato chutney, 1 10 oz. jar sweet pickle, half pint bottle plum or blackberry sauce. There were 28 entries in all with Derbyshire the winners.

1952 saw a new venue for the Annual Council Meeting, Whyte Melville Hall in Fish Street, when Sir Gyles Isham spoke on Vienna, its history and life to-day as he found it on a recent visit. In October the county was back at Towcester Town Hall for the Half-Yearly, where, in addition to resolutions and committee reports, three sound travel films were shown by the County Visual Aids Adviser. These included Inland Waterways, The Royal Canadian Tour, and the Channel Islands.

Miss Minnie Pallister spoke on The Journeys of Celia Fiennes at the Annual Council Meeting on 25th March in the Town Hall, Northampton. Celia Fiennes was a 17th century lady who had travelled all over England on horseback and whose diary was accidentally discovered by a relative, Lord Saye and Seal.

Hey presto, we are out of county for the Half-Yearly Council Meeting which was held in the Assembly Rooms at Market Harborough. A new county badge was launched – a scroll bar, with the wording NORTHAMPTONSHIRE which was intended to be worn under the general WI badge. They were on sale for 1/6d. A County Calendar had also been produced at a cost of 2s. each.

Mrs. Bateson, Chairman of the Denman College House committee, guided her audience through an imaginary course at the College and described vividly the reactions and experiences of an elderly member and her married daughter from another county.

Northamptonshire
and Soke of Peterborough
Federation of Women's Institutes

SPRING PRODUCE EXHIBITION

Assembly Room & Court Room
TOWN HALL, NORTHAMPTON

Wednesday, 30th May, 1951
Thursday, 31st May, 1951
From 10.0 a.m. to 4.30 p.m.

Spring Produce Exhibition – May 1951.

Discussions took place on whether parents should be made financially responsible for wilful damage done by their children to other people's property, and after hearing a local magistrate's views on the subject, the members were in favour of making parents responsible for a sum of up to £5. Regarding Home Help services being developed in rural areas, it was stated that many women were employed in industry, and in any case organised help would not be necessary if people were prepared to help one another.

The entertainment was an Edwardian Play – *Willow, woe is me*.

A new county cloth was proposed and eventually a design by Mrs. Stevens was chosen, although the lettering had to be 'tidied up' by the Art School.

The office was to be closed all day Thursday, and, talking of closing, one WI suspended and one of the decisions it had to make was what was to happen to the bier which was housed in their WI meeting room and presumably belonged to them? Dare I say, heaven knows!

1954 saw Mrs. Cunnington, Long Buckby, in the chair. It had been decided in 1951 that a county chairman should only serve for three years and so we are now getting a quicker changeover.

By 1954 the County finances must have improved as there was a printed agenda for the Annual Council meeting in the Town Hall, Northampton. The large audience of over 300 members were privileged to hear Lady Brunner, the National Chairman, speak on Yesterday, To-day and To-morrow in the WI Movement, outlining its growth and development over more than 30 years, and referring to the interest it had brought into the lives of countless countrywomen. She spoke of the importance of providing a varied and interesting programme and to avoid concentrating on one particular aspect year after year. The future of the Movement would be in the hands of the new and younger members and it would be wise to give them every encouragement. Her inspiring talk was much enjoyed by everyone, and the meeting ended with a dress parade of beautiful gowns from the past 150 years presented by Elton WI under the direction of Lady Proby. The Executive Committee decided to reprint How to Compile a Village History by Joan Wake: 1,000 copies would cost 1/10d. each, selling at 2/6d.

Sadly in July this year the Executive Committee were standing in memory of Lady Denman. There must have been much sorrow at the passing of such a wonderful champion of the WI, but she will always be remembered with great affection. Her picture has pride of place over the fireplace in the main hall at Denman College. In addition, with the money raised for the Memorial Fund a Dining Room extension was added to the College.

The Half-Yearly Council meeting held at Towcester Town Hall on 5th October, was attended by 176 members, 88 of whom were delegates. There were no resolutions at this meeting, but several discussions took place –

1) Criticisms of judges at last Handicraft Exhibition, requesting that more detailed reports were required.

2) Difficulties of accommodating children between 11 and 15 until new secondary modern schools were built in rural areas. Such action as was being taken at that time was being taken out of necessity on rather makeshift lines. A programme of re-organisation of existing village schools was being carried out and in some cases the older children were being sent to neighbouring secondary modern schools.

3) Requesting more help be given by VCOs to newly formed WIs.

4) Was it members' preference to have one large Produce Exhibition in Northampton rather than the several smaller area shows? The answer was in favour of the former.

5) Should entries for Handicraft Exhibitions only be staged if 75% marks achieved. Most felt all members would like to see their work displayed regardless of marks, but sub-committee members stated they had very little time after judging in which to do any staging.

6) Was there any value in organising a WI tent at the Peterborough Show in view of lack of support from members? As this meeting was held in the south it was obvious there would be less support than in the north.

These discussions were followed by a talk from Miss S.H. Buchanan, Superintendent Health Visitor on the vital part diphtheria immunisation had played in getting the dreaded disease under control.

After lunch Garden Competition winners were presented with Cups and Certificates by Countess Spencer, following which Sir Stephen Tallent, KCMG, spoke on Some Resources of Rural Life. giving some unusual and interesting facts. Long Buckby then performed their winning entry in the 1953 Social Half-Hour competition following by Executive members performing a sketch. In September it was reported that Mrs. Dickens had been appointed to the National Marketing sub-committee.

The Annual Council meeting at the Town Hall, Northampton in 1955 was attended by representatives from 142 WIs, and in addition to resolutions, discussion took place on whether sufficient interest would be forthcoming to justify starting up the Produce Guild again in the county – this had been disbanded in 1951. The meeting was not enthusiastic about this.

Miss Viola Williams from National spoke on Land, Food and Us. The Keep Britain Tidy Group was formed at about this time in March 1955 by National and more than twenty organisations representing many different interests signified their willingness to join. Although grant aided by the Government initially the Group became independent in 1961 with a full-time secretary working from NFWI offices. The Queen Mother became patron and Lady Brunner succeeded the Princess Royal as president in 1966.

The Royal Show in the summer which was held in Nottingham saw, Northamptonshire, Nottinghamshire, Leicestershire and Derbyshire combining to produce *A Mummers' Play*, and in July we were again discussing the possibility of a printed newsletter. The estimated cost of this would be £9 for 7,000 copies, but again not enough members were interested in buying a copy.

An International Conference was held in September and these became an annual event with different countries being featured each year.

The Half-Yearly Council meeting, held at Wicksteed Park, Kettering on 5th October was well attended by 200 members. The Hon. Treasurer, Mrs. Clarke introduced the subject of a house being bought for the Federation, asking members to discuss this possibility so that it could be voted on at the next Council Meeting. Discussions, which seem to have been the usual format at Council meetings at this time, took place on –

1) Consideration of whether anything could be done to reduce the amount of advertising matter (even goods sent on sale/return) sent out to Institute secretaries.

2) Was it courteous to knit during lectures and demonstrations.

3) Should not sterner punishment be given to persons guilty of cruelty to children.

4) Asking for instruction to be given on the care of the countryside and protection of birds and animals to large numbers of children who had come from the towns to live on the new estates in rural areas.

5) Asking for National AGM to be a one-day meeting – agreed this would save money.

Awards of Cups and Rose Bowls were presented to the winners of the Produce Exhibition, the County Show Challenge Cup and the ACWW Essay Competition.

Mrs. Kevin Walton spoke on Antarctica and showed coloured slides and the entertainment was provided by the members of the Music committee.

It was reported in November that many WIs had adopted families of displaced persons.

The first large event was again the Council Meeting at the Town Hall, Northampton when Madame Boillot spoke on The French Housewife and Everyday Life in France. Discussion took place on hairdressers not cutting boys' hair on Saturdays meaning time lost from school for children in rural areas.

A Yeast Cookery Day was held at Moulton and members appreciated Moulton Days being re- started when they could visit and explore the facilities.

In addition to the Drama Festival there were three day-schools, Light Entertainment being the most popular with 37 WIs being represented.

The Inter-County Show at Peterborough was visited by HM Queen Elizabeth the Queen Mother, and it was reported she was much impressed with the exhibits.

New items for the Denman bedroom were an etching from Irchester and a replacement bed from Lady Macdonald Buchanan.

At the Half-Yearly Council Meeting at the Victoria Hall, Oundle on 4th October, 1956, Mrs. Capron spoke of her visit to the Displaced Persons Camp in Germany at Unterjettingen, which was the Camp which had been allotted to the Federation. All help that WIs could provide should be sent to Mrs. Capron, who would make sure it went to the Camp: Later it was reported that £111 had been sent for the purchase of equipment for the nursery school and for furniture for some of the people in the Camp. Parcels had also been sent.

Here too we first have news of Mrs. Briggs of Weston Favell who had attended Denman on a Cake Icing Course. She was to become a familiar face around the county demonstrating at major Shows and County events, as well as to WIs – yet another member who found the WI a spring- board launching her into a major interest which she followed for the remainder of her life.

Discussions took place on

1) bottled fruit sent for competition and gaining sufficient marks to merit an award on all other points should be opened and tested, as flavour is an important consideration. This would also prevent the same exhibit being shown again another year. The Agriculture committee had consulted National and having been told of their advice members agreed this suggestion was not practical.

Olwen Briggs, Weston Favell, with her prize-winning iced cake.

2) in view of the mischief children get into in certain villages for the want of something to do, a responsible authority should see that well populated villages had a playground and field thus keeping them well occupied. The Secretary of the Northamptonshire Playing Fields Association was in attendance and answered all questions, finishing by giving advice on procedure to be followed to achieve their aims.

3) accommodation for delegates to the National AGM should be arranged by Headquarters, to enable members who had no relatives or friends in London to attend. Agreed this was not practical owing to the many difficulties for National to organise but that the County would, at all times, assist wherever possible.

4) delegates attending the AGM should have their expenses paid by the WIs they represent; the County urges those WIs sending delegates

WI Produce Guild members at Moulton College. Left to right: Mrs. Angus Ferguson, Mrs. Crofts, Miss Strang, Mrs. E.M. Barker, Miss Hirst Simpson, Mrs. Rotherham.

to consider paying a round sum, to be agreed, to cover travelling and other expenses.

5) Urging that steps be taken to prevent the pollution of the River Nene. A letter was read from the Chief Inspector of the Nene River Board stating that everything possible was being done.

Awards were presented including one for the Year Book Cover Design, the first copy of which would be produced in 1957. This was won by Mrs. Chapman of Broughton. Finally Lady Margaret D'Arcy delighted the audience with her talk on Platforms and People, which was appropriately followed by Warmington providing the entertainment.

1957 did indeed see the first Year Book and Annual Report of the Northamptonshire and Soke of Peterborough Federation of Women's Institutes with its contents not dissimilar to those of today's Year Books. That is, there are the sub-committee details, speakers and their subjects

First Year Book published 1957.

and fees, WIs and their personnel and meetings places, advertisements of every kind, the President's Message, who in 1957 was Countess Spencer, DCVO, OBE, and in the early editions the Annual Report and Financial Statement were included. The Hon. Mrs.E.C. Capron, Southwick was Chairman in 1957.

In February various craft schools were held to teach members the techniques of felt work, linen embroidery and making raffia baskets.

On 27th March we were in the Town Hall, Northampton for the Annual Council Meeting with Mr. E.G. Morris of the Ministry of Agriculture, Fisheries and Food giving an interesting and informative talk on animal epidemics – foot and mouth disease and myxamatosis. After the various awards were presented Mrs. Beryl Northcott spoke on Curious Customs and Beliefs around the World, which proved to be a most amusing talk. The day ended with singing and entertainment provided by the Music sub-committee members performing a very original *Ten Green Bottles*. Gayton organised a Victorian Interlude including songs and dances. Mrs. Holt of Elton took over the position of Hon. Treasurer this year and March found many Presidents and Vice-Presidents attending a Tea Party in Northampton.

The acquisition of WI House in Albion Place had been made possible through the generosity of the Hon. Mrs. Macdonald Buchanan who had given the Federation an interest free loan of £2,000 the house costing £1,500 This meant more space for the secretary, Miss Whatley, craft and drama schools could be held there as well as committee meetings and it was close to the main line bus station at the Derngate. Quotations from the builders were £507 for repairs, with £28.15s. later being spent on a sink unit at the top of the house.

Exhibitions were staged at the Peterborough Show, together with a Handicrafts Display of mixed crafts; also different aspects of WI work were exhibited at the Northampton Show, including a display of musical instruments and music suitable for WI use.

A Milk Day was held in the Gas Showrooms with a cheese exhibit by Kinghams and a Milk Bar by the Milk Marketing Board. The afternoon featured a panel of speakers chaired by Miss Strang who by this time had become Vice-Principal of Moulton College.

A National Verse Play Festival was held at Kettering and the Drama sub-committee organised this for the five counties involved. Spring and summer drama schools were held to help WIs with the technical side of acting and producing. The county had now acquired a considerable wardrobe and WIs could hire these clothes, as well as a full set of stage curtains.

A Singing Day in May was taken by Mr. Stephen Vann, Master of Music at Peterborough Cathedral. 50 members attended and were taught madrigal singing as well as given advice on singing and conducting. The County Music Adviser undertook a choir leaders' school in preparation for the Christmas Carol Festival; and an excellent Festival was held at Long Buckby with 20 choirs taking part and a total of 250 singers.

The Half-Yearly Council meeting on 16th October was held at the Town Hall, Towcester, with Mrs. Pat Jacob from National giving an inspiring talk on Science and Ordinary People. Earlier in the month an Any Questions had been held at the YWCA with a panel of speakers answering questions which had been sent in by WIs. The panel consisted of Chairman of Management at St. Crispin's Hospital, Headmaster of Wellingborough School, Chairman of the Northampton Magistrates' Court, and the Secretary of the Northampton Hospital Management Committee. A Florentine Stitch rug was provided for the Northamptonshire Room at Denman and two members attended craft courses there – Mrs. Billings of Moulton Pillow Lace and Mrs. Clarke of Cosgrove Linen Embroidery. Denman at that time was £1 per night including full board. Northampton covered market had been trading for over two years and it was reported that it was fortunate regular customers had found them. The takings were fairly good considering prices for fruit and vegetables had been poor. More soft fruit was needed but the season had been very bad. It was hoped to start a new stall in Corby market but there were no vacancies at that time. A seasonal stall was still running during the summer months at Ravensthorpe which had been quite a successful enterprise.

In January 1958 three former Chairman resigned – Mrs. Lankester, East Haddon, Mrs. Cunnington. Long Buckby and the Hon. Mrs. Macdonald Buchanan, Cottesbrooke. February saw the first meeting of Executive in Albion Place and the new offices were officially opened on 27th May. To quote Mrs Capron –

For some time the search had been going on for suitable premises for the increasing number of WIs in the county – 173 by then. We were particularly attracted by its situation, in a delightfully quiet road convenient for the bus station and at that time with parking spaces in Victoria Parade. But, were the floors strong enough to bear the weight of numbers of WI members – and was the cellar impossibly damp – and would a bathroom on the ground floor, complete with bath, be somewhat in the way? However the problems were solved, and helped by much hard work by members and useful gifts from many

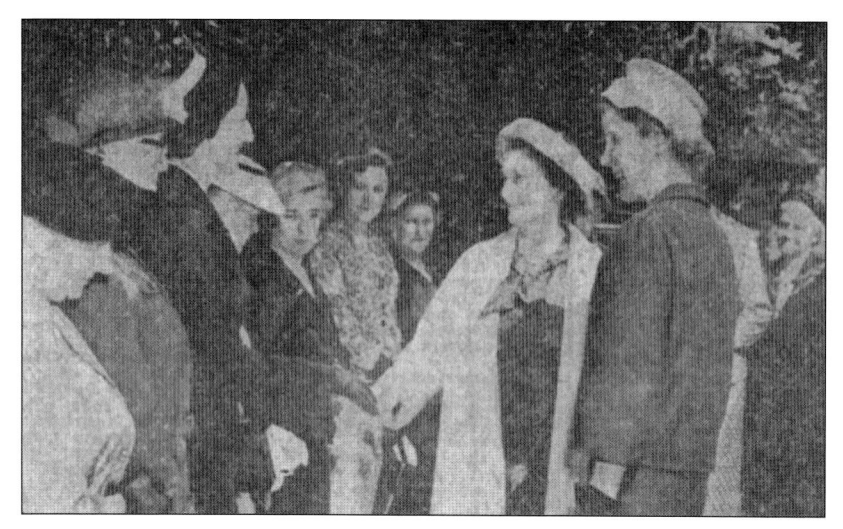

Opening of WI House, 1958 – Duchess of Gloucester and Countess Spencer.

people, the great opening day arrived. It was a beautiful sunny afternoon, and a throng of members made a gay scene (all wearing hats of course) the whole length of Albion Place Our guest of honour, the Duchess of Gloucester arrived, and in a short ceremony on the steps she declared the house open. How proud and happy we were that at last we were the owners of a house of our own – 11 Albion Place, Northampton.

To continue with our diary of events, in February 1958 the first meeting of Executive in the new headquarters was held and arrangements were made for craft schools in glove making, string stools and crochet.

The Annual Council Meeting at the Town Hall, Northampton, on 26th March found Miss McCall giving interesting fact and figures concerning Denman College and Mrs. M. Connell, from National, spoke on the ACWW Conference which had been held in Ceylon. 81 entries had been received for the Programme Planning Competition and Middleton-cum-Cottingham were the prizewinners. *The Farce of the Devil's Bridge* was the concluding item on the agenda and members were then given the opportunity to walk the short distance to 11 Albion Place and view their new headquarters.

Early in May a handicraft conference took place in the Race Course Pavilion when a representative of the Butterick Pattern Company gave

County Show, 1958 – Duchess of Gloucester (right), Mrs. E. Capron, County Chairman (centre).

a delightful and instructive talk on dressmaking. Also in this month a Meat Day was held, in the East Midlands Gas Board Demonstration Room in Northampton when the London Central Meat Company put up a wonderful display of joints and provided a most excellent speaker. There was also a Cookery demonstration by the Gas Board, followed in the afternoon by a Question and Answer session with Miss Strang of Moulton in the Chair.

As already mentioned, on 27th May there were great celebrations when WI House was officially opened and at this time there were 173 WIs and a membership of over 7,000.

Travel has always been popular with members and in June a coach load visited a Carpet factory in Kidderminster. Northampton Show also took place later in this month at Overstone Park and all exhibits were connected with sheep. The county Agriculture and Produce sub-committee produced a collection of different joints of mutton and lamb and also various cooked dishes. Moulton Days continued to be organised when members were able to visit. These opportunities to see at first hand the facilities offered were much enjoyed and the College was thanked for its kind hospitality.

In preparation for the Competition and Concert to be held later in the year, fifty five members attended a Singing Day held at Kettering taken by Mr. Stanley Vann when the work studied was Folk Songs of the Four Seasons. When the Competition and Concert took place eleven choirs competed in three classes. In the evening the Cantata was performed by all the choirs. The Lady Earle Cup was presented by the Countess Spencer to the choir giving the most artistic interpretation of any Test Piece.

A Handicraft Exhibition was held on 24th September featuring 324 exhibits with the Novice Shield being won by Nether Heyford, with Boughton second and Brampton third.

The Half-Yearly Council Meeting at Wicksteed Park, Kettering was the occasion when Lt. Col. John Hills, Lecturer for The Times, delighted his audience with a talk on Our Daily Newspapers The Annual Drama Festival was staged at Glinton, Peterborough for the first time and proved a most successful innovation with performances on four evenings, followed by several at Moulton. Weston Favell won the Novices class and Brixworth, who had won the Novices class the year before this year were the winners of the Open Class.

The Christmas Fair in Northampton in November was reported as being financially successful and a happy occasion.

Another innovation was a Science afternoon when a speaker from Harwell took as his subject Peaceful Uses of Atomic Energy.

An ACWW Essay Competition was held with the winner being Mrs. Beryl Knight of Walgrave. The title was *Things my Grandmother Told Me*. It would be enlightening to print this in full but space does not allow – just one or two snippets –

> For a shilling a man would drive cattle fifteen miles or more in a day and then tramp the long road home again at night. When it rained he would stick his head into the corner of a sack and wear it like a hood. It was all the raincoat he had.
>
> They could buy a big jug of milk for a halfpenny from a farmer's wife. She kept the cream to make butter herself.
>
> Medicines they made from wild and garden herbs, fruits and flowers. They made a plaster of cobwebs to stop bleeding, rubbed earth into cuts to help heal them and charmed warts away by wrapping a piece of raw meat round them overnight, then burying the meat in the garden and as it rotted so the wart rotted too.
>
> A never-failing source of amusement was to put a horse in the shafts backwards whilst its driver was regaling himself in the inn and then to watch with glee his befuddled efforts to drive it when he came out in the dark.

Chapter 7
CHANGES GALORE!
1960–1974

The next ten years or so will see a time of consolidation and new ventures. We still encouraged high standards in cookery, crafts, flower arranging and art, and over the years our participation in the Royal, County and East of England Shows brought many awards to members in the county. Music and Drama continued to play a large part in our programmes, and our appetite for education and knowledge remained undiminished, and we were concerned with all aspects of family life and our environment.

At the end of 1959 Miss Whatley resigned due to ill health; the Assistant Secretary also resigned. The Hon. Mrs. Capron had completed her three years and Mrs. Ethelwyn Tynan of Isham was elected County Chairman. Mrs Joan Battle took on the mantle of Hon. Treasurer from Mrs. Holt of Elton who had left with her husband for Brazil, and Mrs. Battle also held the fort in the office until the appointment in February 1960 of the new secretary, Mrs. Mary Perry.

The Annual Council Meeting took place at the Town Hall, Northampton with 112 delegates attending. Mrs. J. Lightwood spoke on Life in South Africa and a new Co-operative Competition Operation Store Cupboard consisted of home made goods which could be found in any store cupboard, and created great interest.

In April at the Race Course Pavilion Viyella Ltd. of Nottingham held a fashion parade of hand knitted garments and this was followed by three afternoon schools in Northampton and one in Peterborough on Speech and Acting, Production, and Stage Management. To help members with their social half-hours, a singing day was held at Knuston Hall when country singing, rounds, part-singing and percussion bands were the order of the day.

For the three Shows this year demonstrations continued to be given, with Mrs. Briggs putting in a great deal of time and energy to make her cake icing demonstrations a success at the Northamptonshire Agricultural Show, a Co-operative Competition being organised at the Peterborough Show, and a gift shop window displaying a number of crafts being staged at the County Show at Overstone Park. A Handicraft Exhibition at St. Giles' Buildings, Northampton over

Mary Perry, County Secretary, 1965

two days had 380 entries. The Challenge Urn was won by The Bramptons.

The Queen Victoria Hall at Oundle was the venue for the Half-Yearly Council meeting on 7th October, with Mrs. L. Ferguson, OBE, providing an entertaining talk on Learning to Fly at 60 After the presentation of awards for the various Shows and the Gardens Competitions which continued to be held annually, Newborough & Borough Fen performed an amusing play entitled *Six Maids a-Mopping*.

A Christmas Carol Festival was held at Rothwell. 14 choirs took part with a total of 150 singers. The main item was *The Christmas Rose*, a cantata by Thomas Dunhill, which was accompanied by a string quartet and a recorder.

Various surveys were carried out with information being collected from WIs on village scrapbooks, telephone kiosks and areas of demolition of old houses and cottages. The Produce Guild was re-formed and in celebration a most successful tea party and get-together was held at Cottesbrooke Hall, where a Market Stall raised the sum of

£10 Plans were made for the future, with the Hon. Mrs. Macdonald Buchanan in the chair, and Mrs. M Dickens as secretary.

1960 was nominated World Refugee Year, and it was appropriate that Mrs. Capron reported £615 had been collected for Unterjettingen Camp with £415 for other refugees. 17 children, all boys came over for a month's holiday in the summer and were housed with various WI members in the County. The money we had raised meant most of the families from the Camp were moved to new flats near Stuttgart, where they could obtain work. The fund had also helped to buy curtains, lamps and so on for them and had enabled a girl to start college.

Mrs. Capron felt to keep the interest of members we must do new things, and some of these were probably being forced upon us, such as the proposals for changes in borough and county boundaries which would mean looking at WI county boundaries and realigning where possible.. Our National Vice-Chairman, Mrs. Gabrielle Pike, attended the Council Meeting in the Town Hall, Northampton on 30th March and gave a most entertaining and stimulating talk on Our Changing Outlook. The winners of the 1959 Drama Festival, Hardingstone, performed the play *All the Tea in China*.

Schools were held throughout the year for various handicrafts, wine making, flower arranging and in July a Garden Party was held at Milton Malsor Manor House, the home of Mrs. Yorke, a member of the Executive committee and also Vice-Chairman of Handicrafts. Looking forward to 1961, preliminary arrangements were being made for the county rounds of the Country Feasts and Festivals competition organised by National.

In addition to the Half-Yearly Council Meeting at Daventry on 1st October when Mr. Eric Roberts spoke on Behind the Microphone and in Front of the Camera at the BBC, a Gardening Day was held at Cottesbrooke when members were shown how to take cuttings, etc. Arising from this gardening classes were organised at Moulton.

A Painting Day was held and an ad hoc committee was formed to suggest plans for Painting Days in the county in the next two years prior to the National Art Exhibition in 1963. This project had the support of the Carnegie Trust who had been very helpful financially to the WI over many years.

Mrs. Monicreff Dickens was by now also Chairman of the Catering sub-committee and very much involved in providing food for the Michaelmas Fair, which had proved successful not only in the money raised but in the good fellowship that was engendered. Mrs. Capron reported Mrs. Battle had been appointed to National's Home &

Country committee, and she continued with her theme of wanting new things, urging members to give themselves a New Look.

The Northampton Market was in its 19th year, and it was also reported that the final results of all the fund raising for the new Headquarters at 11 Albion Place meant the financial position was encouragingly stable. Mention was made of a kitchen being installed to accommodate more members at classes. It was hoped during 1961 more members would also just visit Headquarters and enjoy a cup of tea with Executive, VCOs, and members of staff, Mrs. Perry and Miss Riseley who always had a warm and friendly welcome for all visitors.

Mrs. Hubball of Cranford and Mrs. Fisher of Ashton joined Executive in 1961 and another very well known figure joined their number – Miss Margaret Aspinal who at that time lived at The Moorings in Park View, Moulton. She was a member of Overstone & Sywell.

A Members' Room was very much in the minds of the committee. Funds raised by two coffee mornings and a Dress Parade helped to make this possible. Mrs. Felicity Jones was painting a mural and an architect helped to plan the arrangement of the room which it was felt would increase the At Home feeling. It had been useful to have our own kitchen where small groups of members had been able to have personal tuition and actual practice in culinary arts leading to taking Preservation Tests, etc.

It was reported that Northamptonshire had won a National Bursary for being the county whose subscriptions to Home & Country had increased the most, Boughton WI being the individual winners.

Members were told they should take pride in the excellence of work displayed at the East of England Show at Peterborough and at the County Show at Overstone Park.

Congratulations were extended to the Agriculture and Horticulture committee whose members had organised the county rounds of the National County Feasts and Festivals Competition. These were held at the YMCA in Northampton and the Technical College in Corby. Nine exhibits were staged and the standard was remarkably high The winning entries would go forward to an Area Centre in Leicester on 3rd October 1962 and these were 1) Irchester 2) Broughton and 3) Wakerley and Barrowden, and Easton-on-the-Hill.

In 1961 the Drama Festival moved around the county and continued to be held every eighteen months. In order to revitalise the interest in drama a new idea was launched to have a non-competitive festival in village halls around the county. The response was excellent and each night saw a capacity audience. However, after a further two festivals, drama took on another form and the ten-minute competitive events were born. These were held in area rounds at Group meetings, and entries judged went on to a final for the eventual winner to be decided. It was reported that Mrs. Fuller, Moulton, chairman of the Drama committee, whilst having no 'legitimate' drama training, had had drama connections over 17 years in various forms. She had watched with great interest the progress of drama in the WIs and, to quote her, said "This type of hobby helps those of a retiring nature and gives them self-confidence. For those who are artistically minded it is a new way of expressing this temperament – another venue to be explored by WI members whose first interest must be in their homes and with their families. The more you put into a thing the more you get out of it, and this is especially so in drama".

A very special meeting, or rather sherry party, was held in Albion Place for the heads of the Council and its departments, for the representatives of the Rural District Councils Association, the Parish Councils Association, the Rural Community Council and the many other Associations with whom we had worked and to whom we were extremely grateful. This event was catered for by the newly formed Catering committee, which although still in its infancy liked to feel that they were quite successful. Most of the baking was undertaken by the committee members themselves, and therefore only nominated major county events could be helped in this way, which did in fact lead to WI funds benefiting from their efforts.

For the Moulton Days this year there were over 540 applicants for only 140 places, so popular had these demonstrations become. This time they featured Cake Icing, Christmas Cracker making, Veal Cookery, followed by a talk on Plants and Vegetables.

The Music committee reported on two Christmas Festivals at Kislingbury and Oundle when about a hundred singers took part in each. No mention is made of who they were, but it was reported that the choirs were fortunate to have among their number three soloists with lovely voices.

Another innovation for 1961 was the scheme by which the fifty delegates from Northamptonshire to the National AGM in London travelled together and were met at London stations by VCOs and were shepherded to and from the Albert Hall and several hotels. This apparently encouraged a number of newer, younger members to "go to town". This practice must have continued because I remember Mrs. Pauline Duff, with her inimitable humour, describing the crocodile of members she led to one AGM and the fun they had!

The two Council meetings were again held and on 12th April in the Town Hall, Northampton, Lady Dyer gave a most stimulating and witty talk on Looking Ahead, and at the Half-Yearly meeting on 7th October at the Technical College in Corby discussion groups were held by first of all dividing the meeting into two groups and asking a Group Leader to summarise their findings. The subjects discussed were The National, the County and the WIs, the WI subscription and how it is shared, Youth, Telephone Calls – alterations to charges- and finally The Inadvisability and Dangers of Leaving Children in Cars. The speaker in the afternoon was Lady Zoe Hart-Dyke, who, after presenting the various trophies, gave a hilariously funny but most informative talk on silkworms and silk.

Various members had attended Denman on receiving county bursaries and Mrs. Woodruffe of Badby & Fawsley sent in the following interesting recipe as a result of her visit to the College: Take equal quantities of the following ingredients and blend smoothly together –

1) Calm, quiet dignity – Country house type
2) Efficient organisation in catering and comfort – First class hotel type
3) Purpose and knowledge – Executive and VCO type
4) Eagerness and awareness – Young Women's College type
5) Friendliness and sociability – Older WI type

This mixture is thoroughly recommended to all WI members, to be taken as frequently as possible, particularly by those who:

a) wonder whether it is still worth while being a WI member
b) have been a member for years and need re-vitalising
c) are willing but terrified takers of office
d) who avoid meetings on AGM Agenda because they feel them a boring waste of time
e) wonder if anything ever comes of endless resolutions
f) wonder if WIs are becoming jaded or outmoded
g) are eager to improve their knowledge of a craft
h) feel a need to widen their horizons.

The name of this wonderful mixture? DENMAN

Mrs. Fisher, Ashton, chairman of Public Questions and Mrs. Fuller, Moulton, chairman of Drama both resigned in 1962 having been a source of strength in their particular fields. A Doris Hart Trophy for Handicrafts was purchased in her memory subscribed to most generously both by individuals and by WIs throughout the county. Mrs. Hart, Harlestone, had been Chairman of both Drama and Crafts committees.

At the Annual Council Meeting on 11th April Lady Spencer had remarked that it was gratifying to the organisers that most county events had been over-subscribed, and she announced that the Members' Room would be opened on 18th April. It was also announced that the County Council grant had been increased from £250 to £400 and that a Prize Draw would be run during the summer. This had meant the year, which had looked like being very difficult from a financial point of view as expenses had increased considerably, would end on a much brighter note. A speaker from National gave a most interesting and informative talk on the Freedom from Hunger Campaign. The Executive committee had completed the day with an entertainment including a performance of The Toy Symphony.

A new committee had been formed, INTERNATIONAL, under the chairmanship of Mrs. Peart, The Bramptons, whose remit had been to encourage support for the Freedom from Hunger Campaign. An International Day had also been organised with one speaker talking about the Campaign and another talking about Displaced Persons in Germany.

Garden parties had been held at Whittlebury and Southwick – at Whittlebury there had been part songs, choral solos, folk dances, country dances, national dances in costume, singing games and handbell ringing, whilst at Southwick the programme included part songs, spirituals, morris dancing, Elizabethan dances (old and new) and a percussion band.

The Half-Yearly meeting held on 6th October at the YMCA in Northampton heard the sad news that Lady Spencer was resigning as County President after 30 years. Discussions took place on limiting expenditure on staging at the Peterborough and Overstone Shows, and although Miss Aspinal stated she thought this would be difficult to enforce the majority of the delegates were in favour. Hargrave wanted to see handles on the inside of telephone kiosks; Hardingstone wanted to have names on farm gates in out of the way places; Duston wished the Northamptonshire and Herefordshire rooms at Denman College could be connected, thus making one large room; Geddington wished to have a revision of hospital appointments and finally Mrs. Battle led a discussion on the Panel of Speakers, all in all a very busy morning. The talk in the afternoon was on Africa and the entertainment was in the form of songs by Gilbert and Sullivan, a monologue and hand bell ringing.

The county Art Exhibition was held on 13th October at the Northampton School of Art and was opened by Lord Spencer, whose appreciation of creative work was warmly expressed. There were a large number of entries and forty awards were made in the various classes. From these nineteen entries went forward to National's Painting for Pleasure exhibition held in 1963. 1963 saw the county preparing for two major events, namely, the Royal Show in 1964 and the National Jubilee in 1965, and to make the necessary arrangements two ad hoc committees were appointed. We were also involved in discussions on the new Boundaries which would affect the county in 1965, as well as railways closures.

There were a few changes in personnel with Countess Spencer retiring, and the Hon. Lady Macdonald-Buchanan being elected to succeed her. Miss Margaret Aspinal took on the role of Hon. Treasurer from Mrs. Joan Battle who having been appointed to National Executive, became National Treasurer and Mrs. Monicreff Dickens also decided to retire from Executive although remaining on her committees of Marketing and Agriculture & Horticulture. It was said of her, that in addition to missing her experience on Executive, her amusing forecasts of what members were likely to think, her common sense and, above all, her wit would also be missed. At the Annual Council Meeting on 3rd April 1963 Lady Spencer was presented with an illuminated book giving all the names of WIs with their love and gratitude.

The back garden of WI House was concreted to keep it tidy, although the large apple tree in the centre was saved, as well as the garage at the bottom of the garden. The grant from the County Council continued to be £400 with the addition of a Peterborough grant of £45.

The Northamptonshire room at Denman College was re-furbished making it look much brighter and more cheerful The new soft furnishings had been made by members of the Handicrafts committee. By this time Northamptonshire had been allocated a room in Brunner House which is particularly noteworthy in that the room had been designed with the needs of the handicapped student in mind, with wider doors suitable for a wheelchair, and lever taps, etc.

Northamptonshire gained second place in the Huxley Cup competition which is for a flower arrangement and is open to all counties and staged at the Royal Show. Our arranger was Mrs Burt, Harpole.

Mrs. Davidson, Duston, was elected Chairman in 1964 and at the Annual Council Meeting on 18th April, reported on the Home Safety Quiz which had been televised and was won by Croughton. The Royal Show, for which the stalls and displays had been jointly staged by

Northamptonshire and Leicestershire & Rutland had been greatly praised and had the honour of being visited by the Duchess of Gloucester and the Princess Royal. The exhibits involved a great deal of planning which had been undertaken by the ad hoc committee under the chairmanship of Mrs. Mackaness, Boughton. A profit of over £100 was made which was to be spent on repairs and decoration of Albion Place.

A competition for increased membership was won by Pipewell & Rushton, and over 300 members attended a Christmas Decorations event at the YMCA.

Early in 1965 Winston Churchill had died, the Death Penalty was abolished, Julie Andrews starred in the *Sound of Music*, and yes we had the mini skirt.

This was National's Jubilee Year, and Mrs Joan Battle, Hackleton & District who took over the reins in Northamptonshire was delighted to welcome Mrs. Gabrielle Pike, National Chairman, to the Annual Council Meeting on 31st March. Mrs. Pike spoke on the Jubilee and afterwards which inspired members to begin the next 50 years with optimism. After the meeting members had the opportunity of talking to Mrs. Pike and members of the Executive Committee.

National's Golden Jubilee Year was celebrated in Northamptonshire in a number of ways. First of all, flower beds in the form of the WI badge were planted by the local councils at Wellingborough, Kettering and Corby.

A Reception was held in February, but sadly, because of an accident the Duchess of Gloucester was not able to attend. By way of a telegram she sent a message of good wishes to the guests who included two members from every WI, dignitaries from various authorities and organisations, and past members. The Earl Spencer, Lord Lieutenant of the County, welcomed each guest personally, and with music from the Minstrels' Gallery, flowers, sherry, delectable refreshments, and a delicious Jubilee cake, made by Mrs. Briggs of Weston Favell it was a happy and memorable evening.

The National Chairman had spoken at the 1965 Council Meeting, and this was followed on 22nd May with Northamptonshire's main event which was held at Grendon Hall and consisted of a Pageant based on the lives of a number of remarkable women in the county, and showed how their various qualities gradually developed into the twentieth century image of emancipated womanhood. It was entitled *The Changing Image* and featured twelve different periods from Boadicea AD60, who is thought be buried in Whittlebury Forest to the

Last Witch in Northamptonshire AD 1785, finishing with The Twentieth Century Image – a brief account of the WI movement. Mrs. Gordon, Duston had taken the script produced by Mrs. Alan Turner and produced and directed the whole affair. Mr. Edward Stober, was thanked for the excellent recorded sound effects and Mr. Gilbert Gordon for the narration, both being WI husbands.

Two performances took place of the *Folk Songs of the Four Seasons*, a cantata for women's voices which was written by R. Vaughan Williams for the NFWI, and was given its first performance by Massed Choirs of the Federations at the Royal Albert Hall, London, in June 1950. They were given by choirs from Broughton, Cogenhoe, Collingtree, Flore, Kislingbury, Middleton-cum-Cottingham, Southwick, West Haddon and Whittlebury. These were attended by over 1,000 people at each performance listening to the 100 voices of the massed choirs. Golden Jubilee glass goblets were for sale. These had a WI badge in gold on the side, and many WIs probably still have them. Other items for sale were a jubilee book,, tea towels and recipe book, and last but not least a rose which had been specially produced by Harry Wheatcroft – a salmon pink floribunda, which was to appear first at the Chelsea Flower Show in 1966.

A competition was launched for WIs to compile a Village Scrapbook about life in their village, these books to be judged at county level and then one from each county would go forward to National for final judging.

Membership in Northamptonshire stood at 7,420 and it was the second year running that this had increased by more than over 200 over the previous year.

Two flights were organised, one to the Dutch bulb fields and the other to Paris. 114 members went on the Dutch trip which cost £9. 9s, and the Paris trip which ended with a champagne supper on the return flight was £9.15s. Two planes were chartered for the popular Paris trip on 7th May.

One event that every WI has written to me about and a souvenir of which they have all saved, is an invitation to all Presidents to the Royal Garden Party at Buckingham Palace on 31st May, from 4 – 6 pm. Members were requested to wear Afternoon Dress and Hat.

The National ruling on not being able to form WIs where the population is greater than 4,000 was rescinded and from this time they could be formed wherever there was a wish for a countrywoman's organisation. This National AGM was attended by HM Queen Elizabeth the Queen Mother.

CHANGES GALORE! 1960–1974

> E II R
>
> The Lord Chamberlain is commanded by Her Majesty to invite
>
> Mrs K. V. Oller
>
> to an Afternoon Party in the Garden of Buckingham Palace to mark the Golden Jubilee of the National Federation of Women's Institutes on Monday, the 31st May, 1965, from 4 to 6 o'clock p.m.
>
> Afternoon Dress with Hat   (Weather Permitting)

An invitation to the Royal Garden Party at Buckingham Palace, May 1965.

Members in Northampton leaving for Buckingham Palace, 1965.

At the County Show at Overstone two kitchens were staged, a 1915 one and another for 1965. By the end of 1965 another major change had taken place in the County in that we had lost the WIs in the Soke of Peterborough as the 11 WIs involved had decided they wished to be transferred to Huntingdon & Peterborough Federation (see list in Appendix). It obviously made a great deal of sense for them to do this as their headquarters would be based at Huntingdon and many of their major meetings would be in Peterborough instead of Northampton. At the Council Meeting Mrs. Battle had reported that this transfer was a sad loss to Northamptonshire but they were wished well in their new sphere, and thanked for their support in the past. The Council Meeting on 2nd April 1966 followed the usual format except that instead of a speaker in the afternoon there was a first public performance of a short extract from *The Brilliant and the Dark*.

A new departure was the holding of the Yalf-Yearly Council meeting in the evening of 5th October and on Mrs. Battle asking for a show of hands it was seen that almost all the delegates had never previously attended such a meeting. Obviously the need for an evening Council had been fully endorsed. The speaker from the Planning Office gave an absorbing talk on Village Planning in the County.

Later in the month there was to be a Conference on Mental Health and an Exhibition Day. 1967 saw the *Mercury & Herald* awarding a cup for an annual essay competition. The first title was Characters of my

Mercury & Herald *Literary Cup being presented to Mrs. Jean White, Hardingstone.*

Conducted tour of Billing Aquadrome – Sam Mackaness, 1967.

Village with 1000 to 1500 words. The winners were Gt. Billing with Barton Seagrave second and Kislingbury third. Gt. Billing's essay portrayed members of the Elwes family (who had Denman College connections) to Charlie Tipper the sweep with his clean shirt; also memories of three elderly women aged 80 who were all still living in the same houses in which they were born. One recollection was of handmade lace being 7d. a yard – a yard taking 7 hours to complete, much of it done under the flickering light of a candle. Barton Seagrave's story was of one family over 100 years, whereas Kislingbury described many colourful personalities. The judges commented that the standard of entries was very high, and the best 12 entries were published by the *Mercury & Herald* over the following weeks.

The Annual Council meeting on 5th April were delighted with the talk Thinking Aloud by Mrs. Eliot Warburton, OBE, JP, which was an absorbing and amusing account of some of the cases which had come before her as Chairman of a Juvenile Court in London.

At this meeting it was announced that the Federation had completely repaid the debt on WI House and a special Celebration Day was to be held at WI House on 16th May.

In May also a group of members were taken for a ride after receiving a special invitation to visit Billing Aquadrome. They were given a conducted tour by Sam Mackaness on the 'trailer bus'. 1968 saw Mrs. Mildred Cockram, Stoke Bruerne & Shutlanger, as Federation Chairman and she was to be in charge for the Golden Jubilee Celebrations of the Northamptonshire Federation of Women's Institutes. A special message of congratulation was received from Lady

Jubilee Cake cutting by Earl Spencer, with Hon. Lady Macdonald-Buchanan and Mrs. Joan Battle.

Anglesey, National Chairman. There were 171 WIs in the Federation at this time with 7,242 members.

The Annual Council Meeting held on 29th March was attended by Lady Anglesey who gave an account of her visit to the Carribean. She accompanied this with beautiful coloured slides. At the Half-Yearly Council meeting on 23rd October in the Anglian Building Society Hall Mr. John Snagge had delighted the audience with reminiscences of his work with the BBC. He was followed by an Any Questions session.

Golden Jubilee Day was 29th June and was celebrated at Cottesbrooke Hall, the home of the Hon. Lady Macdonald-Buchanan who was still President at this time. Fine weather drew large crowds to the event although two last minute setbacks had threatened the celebrations. Lady Macdonald-Buchanan fell ill, but the Countess Spencer, who had herself been President for 30 of the WI's 50 years took over and presented the prizewinners with their awards. She toured the show with the guest of honour the Duchess of Gloucester.

Members representing Boadicea at WI Pageant.

The other accident was that one of the main marquees had collapsed before the show when a pole broke under the weight of the rain so that a replacement had to be brought in. There was an international doll display, all having been hand-made, a cake icing competition, a children's art display, and the grand finale was a presentation of excerpts from *Alice in Wonderland*. Set in the Hall's rose garden, the production was light and full of fantasy. Costumes were colourful and traditional. Members from Kettering had performed a Keep Fit display, which had been followed by a programme of music and maypole dancing. Two fortune telling booths were the most popular side-shows of the day.

In 1969 it was the turn of Home & Country to celebrate its Golden Jubilee – Mrs. Cockram was on the National committee – and I have in my possession Dingley & Brampton Ash WI's Golden Certificate awarded to them in appreciation of 50% or more of their members subscribing to the magazine. There being no WI at Sutton Bassett where I live I joined both Dingley and Ashley WIs when I first arrived in Northamptonshire, both being equidistant and both Presidents having invited me to join them. It always caused a great deal of amusement when asked to introduce oneself and I always had to reel off 'Joyce Haynes, Ashley with Weston by Welland, and Dingley & Brampton Ash WIs' However, I am getting too far ahead as this did not

Finale of WI Jubilee Pageant.

happen until 1975. For over the last two years or so choirs, dancers, actors, etc. had been rehearsing all over Northamptonshire, hoping to have the opportunity to appear in the grand opera called *The Brilliant and the Dark*. It was reported that the 1,000 strong choir sang magnificently as the beautifully dressed show went with truly professional zip. Commissioned four years previously from leading composer Malcolm Williamson and described as an operatic secret, it depicted the place of women over 1,000 years whilst the men went to war.

Two performances were given in the Royal Albert Hall on 3rd June and 11th July and were sold out and it was said to have unearthed a wealth of talent. Among the audience was the Duchess of Kent, herself a member of Iver, Buckinghamshire.

Northamptonshire's Mrs. Joan Battle was the Festival Organiser and she had been one of the accompanists at our own County Music Festival on 27th April at the Carnegie Hall in Northampton, the other being Mrs. Hulbert of Gayton.

An Inter-County Tennis Match was held at Burton Latimer on 12th July between Northamptonshire and Cambridgeshire and later a beautifully illustrated certificate was presented to the winners – Northamptonshire.

For the two Council meetings this year, the speakers were Mr. J.P. Brooke-Little, the Richmond Herald of Arms who delighted everyone with his knowledgeable and highly entertaining talk on Ceremonies, and Mr. Paul Jennings who had talked about the village scrapbooks.

Royal Albert Hall, 1969. The Brilliant and the Dark *seamstresses.*

A Countryside Day was held on 29th October when members intending to walk to the event in he Guildhall, Northampton were asked to notify Miss Lismore of Culworth, another of Northamptonshire's dedicated workers, in order that seats could be reserved for them. Walks were to start from five venues around Northampton.

Before the Day members had been asked to complete a Questionnaire and the results of these were to be analysed for everyone to see, giving helpful advice on how to take action on the various problems that had been raised on Water pollution, Scheduled buildings, Tree Preservation orders, Natural history and Planning applications.

1970 was to be European Conservation Year, and a nationwide competition This Green and Pleasant Land was launched. An Area Conference was to be held at Corby.

Early in April the Report of the ad hoc committee on the Constitution and Rules was published and various recommendations made which would mean resolutions being presented to the members for consideration for a National Annual Meeting in due course. Three previous reviews had taken place, which had resulted in some changes in 1924, 1928 and 1945. 1924 alterations became necessary because of changes in financial law, and the others related to – area representation on National Executive, National Council to replace National Executive, the function, size and composition of the Annual General Meeting, the Consultative Council, etc and all had come before the members in the form of resolutions.

On 22nd April at the Annual Council meeting Mrs. R. Miller from the National Farmers' Union had spoken on the economics of the Common Market, after which it was agreed that an expression of opinion should be forwarded to the Government, urging that more information should be made available as to its effect upon the farming community and the housewife. Miss Christina Foyle was the afternoon speaker on Bookselling, and she gave a witty and informative talk which delighted the members. West Indian songs and Indian dances completed this eventful day.

An unusual topic for the speaker at the Half-Yearly Council meeting on 28th October was Witchcraft given by Dr. Webster. It was said to be most absorbing, and had held the members spellbound! Members heard of the success of the two performances of *A Midsummer Night's Dream* on 2nd October at the Northampton Technical College. There was a choir of 150 members formed from 20 different WIs. During the past six months they had been rehearsing with their own conductors and had done so well that they only came together for one day prior to the full dress rehearsal. Mr. Malcolm Tyler, music adviser for Northamptonshire conducted the performance. The drama side of the production came under Mr. Gilbert Gordon, Northamptonshire's drama adviser, and his wife who was a member of the county drama committee.

We have some new committees, **COUNTRYSIDE**, **HOLIDAYS**, **PUBLICATIONS** and **PUBLIC QUESTIONS**, all of which will show the way the WI is changing With them we also find new Chairman, many of whom you will have either have met or heard of during your WI membership. Firstly, Mrs. Rebecca Westaway of Naseby chaired Countryside, Mrs. Mary Hawkins of Weston Favell Holidays, Mrs. Luck of Lt. Houghton Publications and Mrs. Twemlow of Welford Public Questions.

On 31st March 1971 at the Annual Council Meeting in the Guildhall, Northampton, Mrs. Pauline Duff, Scaldwell, who was this year elected Federation Chairman, welcomed Miss Sylvia Gray MBE, National Chairman. Miss Gray stated that now that all doors were open to women it did create responsibilities and we had a duty to educate

WI Choir, with pianist Joan Battle.

ourselves so that when we were asked to give our opinions they were well informed. This was particularly so in view of the modification of the non-party political, non-sectarian Rule, which was so often being broken. We had to hand over the movement to the next generation with their new thinking to enable them to go into the next 50 years with confidence.

The next speaker was Miss Barbara Walton, Arrivals Officer of the Northampton Development Corporation who told the members this body had been set up by the Government to work alongside the Council to increase the size of Northampton by 100,000, and explained how this was being done to the best advantage of everyone.

The afternoon speaker was Miss Susan Swanton, who enchanted and amused members with her talk Is your Complex Inferior? Brackley Choir provided the entertainment.

This was the year we elected a new County President to take over from the Hon. Mrs. Macdonald-Buchanan who had retired after 6 years, although she had been County Chairman prior to that as well as chairman of the Produce Guild, and of Agriculture, Horticulture and Marketing. This is when Mrs. D.S. Cockram started her long term of

*Lady Macdonald-Buchanan being presented with her retiring gift by
Mrs. Mildred Cockram, who was to follow her as President.*

office. Another familiar name, Mrs. Winnie Shurville, Weston Favell, chaired her first Catering committee, Mrs. Doris Clark, Evenley, Music, Mrs.Briggs, Weston Favell, Drama and Mrs. Toseland, Pipewell & Rushton, Organisation.

A Golf Tournament was held on 4th June by kind permission of British Timken, and a Bowls Tournament was held at St. Crispins in September . Table tennis and Swimming instruction were two further avenues to be explored.

The Half-Yearly Council meeting was held at Bugbrooke School on 30th October, when Mr. John Wilson, the Director of the Royal Commonwealth Society for the Blind, gave an amusing talk on his work. A new item, Personally Speaking, was introduced in which members described experiences they had enjoyed through their WI membership, ranging from attending a Royal Garden Party to a session on the Tempsford Skidpan. Folk singing and poetry to a guitar accompaniment formed the entertainment.

Into 1972 with the sad news that Countess Cynthia Spencer had died. 26th April we were back at the Guildhall for the Annual Council Meeting, with Mrs. Pamela Chatworthy giving an illuminating talk on Life with Mother – Gertrude Lawrence.

The quarterly magazine *Round-Up* was started under the editorship of Miss Ashmore, Brington followed by Molly Bedford, Cold Ashby, Ann Purser, Lois Weedon & Weston, and Freda Richards, Weston Favell, this continuing until 1984.

The East of England Show was to have The Common Market as its theme, and a dressed doll competition would be organised, dolls to be bought in bulk and costumes to be only of Common Market countries. Central display to show East of Britain and Northamptonshire were to stage the south and south-west of England.

The Half-Yearly at Wicksteed Park, Kettering on 25th October featured Alistair Scott Johnstone giving a most entertaining and amusing talk on The Perils of Earning a Living in Comedy. It was reported that the meeting ended with an excellent buffet supper, costing 25p per head.

1973 was Architectural Heritage Year which was a campaign to awaken people all over Europe to the realisation of the loss of irreplaceable buildings and the destruction of the individual character of our towns and villages over the past twenty years, and to halt it before it was too late. A competition would be started in the Autumn so that all members could have a critical look at the buildings and features of their villages, good and bad.

We were especially proud this year when Northamptonshire won the Huxley Cup at the Royal Show and it was presented to Mrs Duff on our behalf at the Royal Albert Hall. The Cup was originally presented to National by a former National Treasurer, Mrs. Gervase Huxley and was awarded annually for a flower arrangement competition held at the Dairy Show which continued until the beginning of the war. It was not held again until 1958 when the venue changed to the Royal Show at Stoneleigh. It was there that talented WI member and well-known flower arranger, Mrs. H.L. Knight, Old, competed for the Cup for a flower arrangement depicting the theme Discovery. Her winning arrangement was in shades of pink and rose.

The initial plans for To-morrow's Heirlooms were started this year and the Town Hall booked for 24th August 1974 for staging the county competition where items would be selected to go forward to National when coaches would be arranged to visit the Exhibition.

The two Council meetings had been held on 25th April and 25th October respectively.

At the Guildhall, Lady Cayley had spoken on Eve to Elizabeth II and there had been delightful singing by members of the Music committee. At Daventry, Mrs. Betty Penny had spoken on Memories of a Mayoress. It was reported that Kettering Market was open on Fridays from 14h July in Vicarage Drive off Market Square, and that Towcester was having an 'up and down' time.

There had been a Table Tennis Tournament at Doddridge Hall in January, a Swimming Gala at Duston in March, a Golf Tournament in April at Oundle, and coaches had been organised to visit Ladies' Day at Ascot in June.

In 1974 Mrs. Wendy Bowler, Mears Ashby was elected Chairman and for her first Council Meeting at the Guildhall, Miss Polly Elwes was a splendid speaker on How to combine a career, husband and family and keep sane. Gt. Houghton Prep school choir had performed at the end of the meeting. The Half-Yearly meeting was held at Wicksteed Park, Kettering, on 30th October when the Duke of Grafton talked about Architectural Heritage Year.

A SPORTS committee was finally appointed with Mrs. Jane Rushton, Gt. Billing as its first chairman.

The WI comes to Town was the title of a fair held at the Town Hall, Northampton, at the end of the year, and it was at then also that I was appointed a VCO – Voluntary County Organiser in Surrey. The subscription by this time was £1.00.

Chapter 8
PROMOTION
1978–1989

We have been recording our history over the past chapters, and now that we are in 1975 the organisation certainly begins to look to the future with possible changes to the Constitution, and Promotion Year both in the offing.

As 1975 was National's Diamond Jubilee Year, as part of the celebrations a reception was held at the Drapers Hall in the City of London on 21st January. Five delegates from Northamptonshire were lucky enough to be invited and arrived by mini-cab where they ascended a lovely staircase to be greeted by Mrs. Pat Jacob, National Chairman. After refreshments, they circulated amongst the many guests one of whom was Mrs. Barbara Castle. Members were allowed to wander through the beautiful rooms and Mrs. Duff recalled admiring all the Guild treasurers, particularly the magnificent chandeliers and a very attractive bronze head of Prince Charles.

Mrs. Pauline Duff, County Chairman, with members of Millbrook.

Mrs. Sally Lewis, Braybrooke, with Tomorrow's Heirloom exhibits, 1975.

The setting on 6th March for National's Tomorrow's Heirlooms crafts exhibition was the Art Gallery of the Commonwealth Institute. The theme 'Time' was interpreted as a series of paper sculpture flowers in silver, a floral clock, each flower said to open or close at a set hour of the day and to have been a feature of nineteenth century formal gardens.

The event was attended by HM. Queen Elizabeth, the Queen Mother, referring to herself as President of Sandringham. She was presented with a gold embroidered royal blue silk box. Northamptonshire was well represented among the exhibits which were judged as the finest of the craft work submitted from WIs throughout the country. All exhibits had to have received 90% minimum marks at their county exhibition. Our exhibits were transported to London by Mrs. Sally Lewis, Braybrooke, who had four entries selected.

Mrs. Jacob did attend Northamptonshire's Annual Council Meeting on 30th April, when Brackley gave a performance of *Noah and his Floating Zoo*.

A Down to Earth event was held at Holdenby House on 14th May, which gave members a unique chance to find out how to make the most of both garden and greenhouse and how to Grow, Gather and Gain. This must have been the start of the popular events with this name which were taken round the villages in Northamptonshire for many years when members opened their gardens and refreshments were available.

1975 was also International Women's Year, so a Commonwealth Countries evening was held at Sponne School, Towcester on 19th May, the Sports committee gave a Garden Party at Cottesmore, Great Billing Park and the main county event of the year was the Diamond Jubilee at Cottesbrooke Hall on 5th July. Here Mrs. Edith Gordon produced the third of her own productions for a county event This time it was *Through the Looking Glass*. For the first time music was included, and members turned into chesssmen on a giant size chessboard. Their costumes and those of the other actors made a colourful and exciting contribution to the production, and they were made and designed Mrs. Doreen Capell of Weston Favell.

Three day educational tours had been started by Mrs. Shurville, Home Economics, and Mr. Phillips of Moulton College in 1974 and this one was to be based in Sussex. On the way down members visited the home of Sir Felix and Lady Brunner at Greys Court. Lady Brunner you may remember was influential in getting Denman College off the ground. The party were to stay at the Dolphin & Anchor at Chichester, and they arrived in the evening. In the early hours of the morning they were awakened by the fire alarm and, adorned in an assortment of rollers and hairnets, were told to assemble in the lounge. Firemen and policemen were soon on the scene but fortunately it all turned out to be a false alarm, the smoke detector having gone off by mistake.

Next day the Roman Palace at Fishbourne was visited as well as the Upper Weald Museum, and as was usual on these trips a garden was fitted into the itinerary, this time Leonardslee Gardens near Horsham.

A National WI Quiz was played between 16 county teams on a knock out basis, and each county was invited to submit a team of three members. Interested Northamptonshire members were invited to WI House to answer a batch of questions provided by the BBC. About 12 members attended this session and from these three were chosen. Mrs. Hilary Aslett from Pattishall, who was one of them said she was lucky as she had watched Mastermind two weeks previously on which some of the questions had been asked. However, the three team members were Hilary, Mrs. Elizabeth Coxon, King's Sutton and Mrs. Ruth Leach of Gt. Brington. Sadly Ruth was too ill to attend the final Quiz so Mrs. Hilary Young, Wootton took her place.

All recordings were at The Paris Studio in Lower Regent Street, London, so a coach was hired to take the team and a goodly number of supporters, family, friends and members to make the journey easier. Jimmy Young was the question master and we played East Sussex in the first round eventually getting through to the final where we played Northumberland. There were 7 rounds in each Quiz, 3 mixed general knowledge, 2 specialist, 1 great gamble on your own county, and finally a free for all – 20 easy questions, the first to buzz. To their immense delight at the end of the final Hilary, as captain of the team, was presented with a suitably inscribed silver salver which is hung in the committee room at WI House. They were also presented with red carnations and green foliage by the county. After several photographs they were entertained by the BBC at a wine and cheese party. The most outstanding memory of this occasion to the team was the tremendous support they were given by everyone. Their comment was 'they were with us all the way'.

Mrs. Mary Perry retired as county secretary at the end of 1975 and she was succeeded by Mrs. Kathleen Pinton, who attended her first council meeting in this capacity on 28th April at the Guildhall. Mrs. Perry was presented with an embroidered and inscribed book from members. This too was my first meeting in Northamptonshire, the speaker at which was Mr. Eric Nicholson on 'The Art of the Comedian', and guess what, yes, being the new girl, I was asked to thank him. How I ever got up those steps to the platform I shall never know!

In the Autumn we were at Southfields School in Brackley where the speaker was former National Chairman, Mrs. Gabrielle Pike, CBE, JP on Excellent, this will do me very well. This was a talk about the three women who had greatly influenced her life, her Great Grandmother, Mrs. Elizabeth Fry, her own Mother, and Lady Denman.

Sport really took off this year and we had Table Tennis, Tennis, Badminton, Rounders, Darts, Scrabble and a Family Sports day at Lings Forum. Bridge classes were started by Mr. M. Rogers at the YWCA for both beginners and those wishing to polish their skills.

Every year places are balloted for amongst county Chairman for the honour of attending a Royal Garden Party and Mrs. Wendy Bowler was lucky this year and went along on 23rd July with other chairmen, where she reported that promptly at four o'clock the Royal Party appeared. She said the Royal ladies looked pale and elegant and the men fit and bronzed. She came away with happy memories of a very English garden in the heart of London, and of a very pleasant afternoon as guests of fellow member, HM the Queen.

Mrs. Suzanne Palfreyman, Maidwell, was elected County Chairman in 1977 and Mr. Godfrey Talbot was the speaker at her first Spring Council meeting on 27th April in the Guildhall. His talk, I was there at the time, told of some behind the scene experiences of Royal Tours.

Mrs. Suzanne Palfreyman, County Chairman, 1981

Announcements were made of Jubilee events, the Craft Sale at Debenhams (the proceeds of which were to go to the Queen's Jubilee Fund) the sale of 1,000 cakes, and members were asked if they were in favour of a new county cloth being made to commemorate our Diamond Jubilee in 1978.

One chairman refers to emerging from her first Executive meeting clutching the keys of WI House in one hand and the Chairman's badge of office in the other and feeling completely overwhelmed. I am sure every chairman since has had this same feeling, and possibly too those pioneer chairman who seemed to have great resilience and to be particularly strong. One thing we all had in common was the support of a splendid team, both at county and in the county. The Craft Sale at Debenhams resulted in them being completely overwhelmed with nearly 100,000 items for the great sale which raised approximately £25,000. For the Queen's Silver Jubilee we held an Open Day at WI House in May, when members could have refreshments before buying at the grand Bring and Buy stall – nearly new hats, handbags, belts and other accessories, as well as publications.

Another event featured ACWW which Mrs. Olive Farquaharson, OBE, the President attended, and the infamous Sale of 1,000 Cakes at

Sale of 1,000 cakes, 1981 – Joyce Haynes, Anne Smith, Mary Hawkins, June Page and Doreen Chown.

the Guildhall on 21st October. For this latter event the county was inundated with cakes, so generous are members when asked to contribute. However, there are inevitably some cakes that are not quite as saleable as others and a particular tea bread was left at the end of the day. Mrs. Palfreyman who was going to Southwold that evening decided to take this cake with her and feed it to the gulls which she duly did throwing it on the beach. However, she was suitably surprised the following morning to find it still there – even the birds had rejected this one!

At the Half-Yearly Council meeting at Kettering on 2nd November, Mrs. Palfreyman was thanking Gt. Doddington for donating a lectern and gavel. A tremendous number of crafts had been sent to the Debenhams Sale. To the great amusement of the audience, the speaker, Mr. Rupert Spencer told of some of his experiences during his long career as an auctioneer, finishing with producing items which he described and priced. Because of the WI's educational aim it was decided to award a Denman bursary to someone near the Queen's age, that is 45 years plus.

In this year the Keep Britain Tidy Group emerged under its new name having become an independent organisation in 1961 just called Keep Britain Tidy.

1978 was Northamptonshire's Diamond Jubilee, and the first event was held at the Museum and Art Gallery in Northampton from 7th to 10th June. This was an exhibition of paintings selected from those sent in by members. Crafts members displayed their particular crafts in various stages of development, and the beautiful patchwork bedspread made for the Denman bedroom was also on show. The patchwork coverlet was designed by Mrs. Ashmore, Brington, and made with the help of other craft members from 18 WIs as well as the Craft committee. It was entitled 'Cycle of Life' and depicted the four seasons with the twelve signs of the zodiac round the border and Father Time at the foot. On the opening day a lunchtime concert had been organised.

During this year, of course, there were the usual events, the 3-day tour which took members to Avon, Somerset and Wiltshire, the Grow Gather and Gain Day at Litchborough. The Denman College Evening at the Guildhall, when members displayed and talked about the courses they had attended at the College, was a new venture. The year would finish with a Diamond Jubilee Festival Day at the Guildhall and a Jubilee Concert at Nene College, where music from previous events was featured under the title Sing it Again.

We were heavily involved with the East of England (Peterborough) and Royal Shows (Stoneleigh) during this period. Mrs. Duff recalled the many meetings before the shows on wintry days in portable buildings when there appeared to be nothing between the showground and Siberia. Schedules, design, guests and all the other items going into Show preparations were considered in great deal and these were always inter-county occasions, meetings being at a central point. The East of England Show committee consisted of Cambridgeshire, Huntingdon & Peterborough, Isle of Ely, South Lincolnshire and ourselves, each of us taking turns at producing the main theme of the Show and being responsible for chairing the meetings and eventually the Show for two years at a time. We usually had Royal visitors on the Wednesday of the Show, always Princess Alice, then the young Duchess of Gloucester, HM the Queen Mother and Prince Charles. The marquee was always very crowded but members loved the atmosphere.

Northamptonshire was in charge of the catering in one particular year at the Royal Show. This was in the WI pavilion where it was a

East of England – HM Queen Mother with Josie Crisell.

constant battle to keep up with the supply of cold meats, salads, snacks, sweets and drinks. It was pretty exhausting work particularly as the weather was often hot, and therefore it did seem a good idea when preparing food in the secluded yard at the rear to slip off white nylon coats and work in slips. However, an unexpected visit from the dustmen caused a hasty retreat, although it did result in dustbins being serviced pretty frequently for the rest of the week.

Train outings had become very popular, with Mrs. Rae Griffin, Overstone & Sywell on the Travel committee; her husband was a railway employee. Early April found 350 members and families arriving early at Northampton station to travel to York. The following year Canterbury was the destination.

On 28th April 1978 at the Spring Council Meeting in the Guildhall, our National Chairman, Mrs. Patricia Batty Shaw, JP, recalled her days as a member since 1958. She also spoke of the future and said we should not be afraid to voice our opinions, and hoped members felt that money spent on representing them in Europe was money well spent.

Talking of the future, the *Mercury & Herald* competition this year was looking forward and its title was WI 2000. It would be interesting to see some of those entries now and to see whether any of them correctly predicted what has happened.

This year Mrs. Nancy Walker, Grendon, was being congratulated on being awarded the MBE for her work as Warden of Grendon Hall over 20 years, but the year ended with a special gala performance at the Royal Theatre, Northampton. Little did she know that two years later she would be off to the Palace again, this time being lucky in the Garden Party ballot for county chairman to attend.

The Jubilee book, *A County Miscellany*, was being produced by the editorial team of Wendy Bowler, Mears Ashby. Ann Purser, Lois Weedon. and Christine Sutton, Collingtree. After all the excitement of Jubilee year when our membership increased we are back to basics with the Spring Council meeting being held at the Guildhall on 25th April 1979 with our new county cloth on the chairman's table. The dedicated team responsible for making this cloth were warmly thanked, and Mrs. Palfreyman then talked about the opening of the Home Economics Centre by HM the Queen which she had attended earlier in the month with Mrs. Christine Sutton. These places had been decided by ballot and I remember Christine telling me that when she arrived home and told her husband the good news, saying she would need a new outfit, his reply to her was – 'Surely you've got something the Queen hasn't seen!'

Members were thanked for their support during Jubilee Year and mention was made of the Towards 2000 area meetings which would shortly be held following completion of the questionnaires sent out to WIs. The speaker was Mrs Susan Swanton with a talk entitled The Power of the Spoken Word which was excellent and kept her audience entertained in a flamboyant manner as she also acted small items from several plays.

Grow, Gather and Gain went to Ashley this year, and my own WI were very busy producing goods for sale, teas, and putting together an exhibition in School House. Several gardens were opened and a map provided of the village and its facilities.

This was also the year that I was awarded first place in the Gardens Competition, for the Whole garden section. I had a very good vegetable garden then which I had designed and planted and this provided me with a great opportunity to relax at leisure.

We also held 4 Knit-Ins when members got together to knit squares which would eventually be made up into blankets. There were prizes at each venue for the fastest knitters. The knitted strips were eventually made up into 10 blankets for the Save the Children Fund, and a total of £1421 was raised.

The Half-Yearly Council meeting held at the John O'Gaunt Hotel, Daventry, on 31st October was a new departure. Commander M. Saunders Watson talked about the history of his home, Rockingham Castle, which was built by William I in 1066 and was the scene of the first parliament in 1090.

The county Scene 80 Drama Festival took place in September over four sessions. The teams achieved a remarkably high standard and the adjudicator, Miss Joan Fisher thanked everyone for the splendid entertainment they had provided. Eventually the contributions from Long Buckby, (*Tribute*) ,Kilsby (*The Plague*), Mears Ashby (*Sarah*), Moulton Afternoon (*Threat or Promise*) and Moreton Pinckney (*This Human Game*) were short-listed by the National assessors to go forward to the National Finals at Stratford on Avon in July 1980. Prior to this county event a Talk-In had been held at Titchmarsh and a Lighting School and Make-up classes were held to assist WIs in their final productions. All through this lead up and the many hiccups encountered on the way to a successful Festival, Mrs. Ann Dickens, Moulton Aft. had been Chairman of Drama, following a talented line of actresses to take up this position.

Mrs. Nancy Walker took her first Spring Council meeting at the Guildhall on 23rd April 1980. She mentioned the request that had been

Scene 80 – Moreton Pinckney's Chessboard.

received from the Variety Club of Gt. Britain for members to bake and supply 12,500 small cakes for a special day for 12,500 under-privileged and paraplegic children at Billing Aquadrome in June. This worked out at only 60 cakes per WI, and that would be ten members making 6 cakes each, definitely a feasible proposition. As 1980 was the year of the Home Help Mrs. Brown of this service spoke briefly on the way many people were helped in Northamptonshire with approximately 900 Home Helps being employed to help about 3,600 clients. Mr. Dorian Williams was the main speaker, and his talk, Variety is the Spice of Life, kept the audience very amused, and members were surprised to hear he had spent a large part of his youth living at Greens Norton.

Following this meeting WIs were contacted and on the appointed day members of Executive arrived at Billing Aquadrome to receive the cakes – would there be enough? There need have been no worry on that score as Group Conveners kept on arriving weighed down with goodies and some helped with the sorting and stacking. The children's faces when they arrived and on choosing their cakes were a delight to see.

Over the years and with the advent of the Common Market it became apparent that Public Questions and International affairs often overlapped and so a new committee COMMUNITY AND INTERNATIONAL AFFAIRS was appointed, and I was its first chairman. What a challenge. National had much advice on follow-up work on mandates and they frequently asked for members views on particular subjects which they could take to Government ministers. And so the Public Affairs Panel emerged, and members were sent various Green Papers and topics to discuss and report on. The co-ordinator of all these submissions was the talented Mrs. Sheila Masters, Nether Heyford, and a marathon task this was to summarise all members had said. However, Sheila undertook this with great enthusiasm and skill.

The Half-Yearly Council meeting at the Kettering School for Girls, held on Saturday, lst November was certainly something new. Many husbands had taken the opportunity to go along. Discussions took place on Air Rifles in the hands of Juveniles and Disappearing Hedgerows. The speaker had been unable to attend at the last minute but fortunately Mr. Dick Smith, of Chacombe who was in the audience, agreed to talk on Walking the Footpaths and gave members a great deal of information on this subject. An Any Questions session was followed by songs from the 1980's sung and played by Mrs. Ackroyd, Barnwell, Mrs. Clark, Ecton, and Mrs. Fonge, Flore.

The Spring Council meeting on 29th April 1981 at the Guildhall, and mention was made of the generosity of WIs in sending donations for office equipment, etc. WI House was an asset but it needed a great deal of support to keep it in good order for members to visit and use. At that time WIs provided flowers to decorate the various rooms, and also crafts to put in the Showcase. They chose when they wanted to do this and it was wonderful to see some of the results. One addition was a Scroll of Past Presidents and Chairman which had been commissioned from Mrs. Lynne Evans, Denton. She was an expert calligrapher and artist and the Scroll was made possible by a legacy from Miss Lismore, Culworth, who had been a great champion of the WI and held many offices during her lifetime. I provided the second scroll when we ran out of space and so became the first Chairman on this second list. To add to our commitments, the Northampton bedroom needed refurbishment and this was undertaken by Mrs.Winnie Shurville, Weston Favell and Mrs. Doreen Chown, Moulton Aft.

Sadly Mrs. Jane Rushton, chairman of Sports had died, but on a lighter note Mrs. Suzanne Palfreyman was congratulated on being elected to National Executive.

There were two speakers at the Council meeting in the Guildhall on 29th April, 1981; firstly Mr. Gerald Freeman, the editor of the Chronicle and Echo on the Talking Newspaper for the Blind – Sound News, telling members that there were 100 volunteers working on this important county project. Following him, Mrs. Jane Ewart Biggs spoke on being the Wife of a Diplomat At the October Half Yearly meeting at John O'Gaunt Hotel, Daventry, on 22nd October Mrs. Walker reported on the gifts that had been organised for the wedding of Prince Charles and Miss Diana Spencer, who was the granddaughter of our one time President, Countess Cynthia Spencer (1931–1962). These were two table lamps from Yelvertoft with silk lampshades made by Mrs. Mary Pebody, Wootton, a lace collar and a lace-edged handkerchief, both of which were made by members. She told members how my husband had taken us both to London to deliver the presents to Buckingham Palace, how they were meticulously checked in and the constant queue there was of members of the public delivering their presents. At this time also the Federation presented two wall clocks to the Cynthia Spencer House at Manfield Hospital to mark the occasion.

The speaker at this meeting was Mr. David Barby who gave a most fascinating and often amusing talk on the many antiques he had brought with him. The members of the Executive concluded the evening by entertaining members to a peformance of *The Muchado of Life in the WI* – a burlesque based on The Mikado.

At the Annual Council Meeting in Northampton on 28th April 1982 Mrs. Walker spoke about the new National Council which had met for the first time. This conference was a meeting of National Executive committee members with County Chairman and County Treasurers and she felt these meetings would prove to be very productive once the format had settled down.

Miss Aspinal reminded members that we had managed to keep pace with inflation but had quite large expenses to meet in that the garden wall needed re-building and part of the house had to be re-wiring. She thanked members for supporting the County Draw which has raised over £1,000. Mrs. Edna Healey's talk on A Wife at Westminster was fascinating and enjoyable. She told stories and anecdotes of the wives of many politicians and high ranking men from the past to the present day.

The first round of the Driver of the Year competition took place in April and the 25 successful candidates were informed that the County Final would take place at Silverstone Racing Circuit and would be supervised by the Northamptonshire Police. The eventual winner of this competition was Mrs. Judith Pidd of Mears Ashby.

In 1982 I was instrumental in getting sponsorship from J. Sainsbury for two musical events held by National in Bristol and Preston. These were performances of Early One Morning conducted by Antony Hopkins, and my husband and I very much enjoyed our evening at Preston.

The County Fair took place at Grendon Hall on 12th June and featured a special children's corner and races. There were demonstrations of many crafts and arts, stalls showing country activities, the County Youth Band, dancing displays, sales tables with food, plants, kitchen equipment, crafts, and of course there were the usual excellent refreshments. All the WIs and Groups helped with manning the stalls and providing the items to sell.

The Half-Yearly meeting was held at the Festival Hall, Corby on 28th October 1982 and because of the space available it was possible to set up displays of a number of the 'Life in the Community' projects to show members. Mrs. Walker congratulated all the WIs who had taken part as the projects were most impressive and would be of great interest to future generations. Over 60 WIs had compiled chronicles from August 1981 to August 1982 featuring all that had happened in their communities during this time. The Rural Community Council had helped with drawing up the project and the final event was a Countryside Day held at the Guildhall when the then Editor of the Countryman, Mr. Christopher Hall had inspired us to take action in the rural areas if we really wanted them to survive.

She reported that at the last National Council concern had been expressed at falling membership nationally and consideration was being given to a membership drive for 1984. Although the WI was a wonderful organisation with members able to enjoy so many diverse activities, our aim should be to encourage new members as our success in the future depended on our involvement in the community and we should offer our skills and expertise for the benefit of all.

The County Council Grant this year had been £620 and it was hoped this would be continued. The evening concluded with an exciting Fashion Show arranged by Coppers Boutique of Northampton. This was greatly enjoyed by the 900 members present.

Into 1983 and this is where Mrs. Mary Hawkins, Weston Favell, says goodbye and eventually moved to Wales. We welcomed Mrs. Josie Crisell, Croughton, Mrs. Liz Fox, Barnwell, and Mrs. Suzanne Solomon, Gt. Doddington Evg. I remember about this time we often had babies brought to committee meetings with Suzanne, Fiona Harding, Stoke Albany & Wilbarston, and Diana Benarr, Redwell, all delighting us with their various offspring. To think they are now all in their twenties and won't even remember these auspicious outings. Two other members who have become familiar to us all were welcomed, Mrs. Christine Farmer, Preston Capes, and Mrs. Malvina Keech, Cranford.

This was the year I was elected County Chairman and my first outing was to attend National Council in London with the Treasurer, Miss Aspinal where we discussed the Resolutions to be taken at the National AGM in June. We were to attend many similar meetings throughout the next few years and September found us at the 2-day conference in Exeter. We nearly always stayed in University accommodation, so you can see National were being very economical! My first Council Meeting, was held on 27 April at the Guildhall and I took 'Communication' as my theme. There was so much we needed to know about each other at WI, County and National level, and, and also there was much the general public could learn.

Starting with the WIs, I was asked very early in my chairmanship what sort of membership we had and although I knew a great deal from my years as a VCO, I felt I did not know enough. So the idea of a questionnaire was born. Such questions as the usual How long have you been a member, how old are you, what attracted you to join, do you belong to any other organisation, do we cater ror your particular interest, etc. etc. Analysing the results, which showed an excellent return of 95% having been sent to 1500 members we found that over one third had been members for over 20 years, with another third under 5 years. They had joined in the main because it was welcoming when they were new to the area, out of curiosity, for relaxation, stimulation and one unhappy person 'just to get out of the house'. Over 40% were between 31 and 50, 39% 51 to 65 and 18% over 65, and the remainder under 30. 98% were married or widowed and of these 38% had children over school age, with 16% of school age. Only 10% were in full time work with 22% part time. Farmers' wives put themselves into a separate category. Many had thought the WI was about jam making, knitting socks and gossip, but on joining learnt that they were run in an interesting, happy and leisurely way. One thing that did emerge above all else was that WI members certainly have a lovely sense of humour.

The National Federation at its AGM in June had launched its Promotion for 1983-5 homing in on three specific issues, Women in Public Life, Women in Education and Women and Health.

We were asked to brighten up our British Rail stations with flowers and plants, the National Bus company would provide a double decker bus to tour all the Federation and our date would be January 1984 – somebody had to be visited in the snow during winter!

At the AGM at the Royal Albert I had been privileged to represent Northamptonshire to propose the resolution on planning permission for farm buildings being required, bringing them into line with all other buildings. This had been proposed initially by Overstone & Sywell WI but became a County Resolution when it was passed at our Council Meeting. Although this resolution was lost by a small margin our link with the NFU and other organisations became stronger because of it, in that we now have regular meetings. And in fact I met one of my greatest friends through this. He was very vindictive and rude about the WI initially, being secretary of the CLA, (Country Landowners' Association) but once we got together and talked things through we have never looked back. More communication!

This was my Royal Year when I was presented to HRH the Queen Mother, HRH Princess Alice and the young HRH Duchess of Gloucester. All three were members of the WI, at Sandringham and Barnwell respectively.

The new Derngate Centre in Northampton opened in June and to celebrate we held an evening of Music with the County Youth Orchestra and Flowers with John Chennell. At the end of the evening various antiques were valued. £1,700 was raised at this event. A Drama Group Entertainment took place in September with 111 entries. The finals were held at Duston in November, where Yardley Gobion were the eventual winners.

Other events were a train outing to Chester taking 400 members, a Winter Wonderland Craft Exhibition, a Gardeners' Question Time at Moulton College, and Grow, Gather and Gain at Newbottle Manor by kind permission of Lady Juliet Townsend.

At the end of the year we held Link Up meetings at Kings Sutton, Barby, Duston and Geddington to give the results of the questionnaires, to inform and listen to members, and to provide entertainment, which the Executive Committee did with great gusto.

The speaker for the April Council Meeting was Mr. Roy Plomley, whose talk Desert Island Discs kept everyone amused and fascinated with stories of the various people he had interviewed on his long running radio programme.

On 22nd October we were in Spinney Hill Hall, welcoming as VCOs Mrs. Christine Farmer, Mrs. Malvina Keech and Mrs.Anne Mackley. We were saying goodbye to Mrs. Pat Kutas of Milton Malsor for her work as a VCO and also as an energetic Denman College Representative.

The theme of the County for the year was Beautiful Britain, the Queen Mother having launched the campaign in the Autumn of 1982 as Patron of the Keep Britain Tidy Group. I continued with my theme of Communication hoping members were getting involved and allowing themselves to be nominated to new committees. 1984 would be a great challenge to all of us with Promotion being added to our normal calendar, but we would look forward to this.

Joyce Haynes, County Chairman, 1984

Promotion bus, 1984

Mr. Roy Spring talked enthrallingly on Salisbury Cathedral where he was Clerk of Works, and Mrs. Moira Vaughan completed the day when she transported us to the Isle of Man and spoke so warmly about her island with all its folklore, traditions and music.

Finally 1984 Promotion Year arrived and with it the National Double Decker bus. We parked in the Market Square in Northampton and we had many interested visitors both here and at Wellingborough where The Addingtons sang a song set to the tune of Jerusalem and at Kettering, where Jon Beynon of Radio Northampton transmitted his programme from the bus interviewing everyone within sight. What an experience that was! The theme tune of 'Sky High with the WI' echoed everywhere. The respective Mayors came along and opened the Exhibition at each venue. At Northampton, Stoke Bruerne & Shutlanger rang their handbells and the Hackleton & District Keep Fit Group performed for us and inspired members of the public to join in.

At the Council Meeting on 28th March in line with the theme of Communications Continued I announced that a printed newsletter would be launched in the Autumn The cost would be 75p per annum. This year we were showing a surplus of £4,402 on our accounts.

Mr. John Riddington, Chairman of the East of England Show Society answered many questions and he told members that in connection

Hackleton & District Keep Fit Group performing at Cottesbrooke Hall.

with straw burning a new byelaw was being introduced which would alleviate much of the nuisance.

Stoke Albany & Wilbarston were presented with a cheque for £50 as winners of the Community Care competition when they had devised a transport scheme for their area.

Our main speaker was Mrs. Anne Harris, National Chairman, on My job as I see it, stating that. although it was enjoyable and a challenge, promoting the WI was an absolute necessity. We held Open Events at WI House the next day, and many members came along and met the National Chairman who kindly stayed for a marathon morning, afternoon and evening. During the summer WIs held their own promotion events and I was lucky enough to be invited along to see the diversity of ideas and wealth of talent on display, all with a view to acquiring new members.

Early in June many of us travelled to Denman for their Open Week where we were responsible for the catering for three days. Our reward was to receive half of the profit and we made over £2,000. Five of us shared a bedroom, Anne Dickens, Caroline Raven, Winnie Shurville, Christine Sutton and myself and throughout the three days we did not have to change out of our overalls, so busy were we. We provided for 1,500 members, 1,250 requiring set meals and the rest wanting drinks and light refreshments. Huge boilers were housed in the service marquee, tomatoes were ripened overnight in the warmth of our bathroom. No 'health and safety' then, but after all we were all

Catering at Denman – Joyce Haynes and Anne Dickens.

housewives and knew how to bake scones at all hours of the day and night, how to fill 1,800 bread rolls, etc. It certainly was another great team effort – and what fun we had!

The British Home Stores exhibition was held in Northampton over the first fortnight in June, when we were given an excellent corner site. During this time the store kindly put on two Tours and Fashion Shows. Members were also busy collecting till receipts from International Stores which resulted in 287 miles and a cheque for £20,000 being handed over to National for use in our Women in the Community projects.

The highlight of the year was the WI Life and Leisure Exhibition at Olympia, with so many Northamptonshire members providing crafts,

Olympia, 1984

market items, stewards. The many displays and exhibits were exceptional and HM the Queen seemed to enjoy her tour. The Community Quilts were the centre of attraction and here is part of Winnite Shurville's poem after her stewarding;

> Downton Evening, Doynton and Wick,
> Roll up, roll up, and take your pick.
> May I see that, and who made it?
> Is ours sold? I don't believe it
> What is the price range, please they say,
> £20 to £1,000 you must pay
> Single, double, cot size, pram,
> Daughter's flat, or doting gran.
> We the staff would like to breathe
> Please move back and do not squeeze.
> It's Thursday night, our stint has ended
> We journey home with knees 'unbended'
> When County Chairman at next Exec
> Asks for volunteers – oh, what the heck
> Will we again be quite so willing?
> Of course we will however killing!

In October we again visited the Derngate for a Barber Shop performance followed by Vanity Fair's Fashion show. Along with other committee members, I was co-erced into being a model for the evening – from a Frenchwoman with her trench coat and beret to a full length gorgeous pink nightgown, whilst my husband was persuaded to be father of the bride with Christine Sutton as mother.

Finally to end this eventful year Emgas offered to stage a Cookery Demonstration followed by flower arranging with ourselves sharing the profits with the NSPCC. This was held in November with the title 'Christmas starts here'.

What a year – all this in addition to Grow, Gather and Gain at Cottesbrooke, all the usual sports plus orienteering, a train trip to Harrogate and one to the Garden Festival in Liverpool, a Craft Day and other demonstrations and the annual Christmas music event.

I cannot end this year without paying tribute to the Newsletter team. Having suggested the idea I felt I had to take on the editorship, Malvina Keech produced the front pages and other graphics (we weren't so heavily into computers then), Doreen Chown looked after advertisements and Kathleen Pinton undertook most of the typing. The whole thing was a cut, paste and rule up job, but more of that later. Our first front page has been adapted for the cover of this book.

Could 1985 be as busy? Of course it could. This was the Northamptonshire Federation's 70th birthday, and we had formed six new WIs, at the same time celebrating the Diamond Jubilees of six others, Blisworth, Gt. and Lt. Oakley, Guilsborough, Marston St. Lawrence, Milton Malsor and Woodford.

The Annual Council meeting on 20th March, 1985, Spinney Hill Hall, had begun to set the pattern for these meetings to be held in the evening, in that we had more evening WIs, more members were working, and we could seat 750 members as opposed to 300 at the Guildhall. It was at this meeting that the idea of an extension to WI House was launched. The members were asked to make the organisation their charity over the next two years when it was hoped to raise £20,000. More office space was needed, together with more accessible storage space.

Mr. Dick Saunders took us around the course at Aintree describing the exciting occasion when he had won the Grand National on Grittar. Music has always been popular amongst WI members so we were delighted to welcome Miss Daphne Boden, who had been the first British harpist to be awarded the Premier Prix at the Brussels Royal Conservatoire. She had started playing at 4 years old and had studied under Marie Goosens, Marisa Robles and Mireille Fleur.

In May we were celebrating our 70th in the form of two sessions at Turner's Musical Merry-go- Round. Approximately 600 members and friends danced the afternoon and evening away in the nostalgic atmosphere of the mighty wurlitzers and the merry-go-round cockerels and horses. Mrs. Mildred Cockram and Mrs. Monicreff Dickens also took us down memory lane with some of their WI experiences, whilst I received an unexpected kissogram from a would-be sheik.

The Elizabethan Fayre at Grendon Hall in June had great support from Groups who brought and manned the many stalls of the period. Members wore costume, listened to madrigals, and watched a play and also maypole dancing. There was a fancy dress competition for the children and the Crafts committee members had donated a superb patchwork bedspread for the raffle.

Miss Aspinal and I travelled to Durham University for National Council and were saddened to hear of the possibility of closing Denman College. Much discussion took place but we were delighted to hear later in the year that the decision had been taken to keep the

College and an appeal for one million pounds was launched. The idea was to bring the College up to hotel standards so that other organisations/conferences would be prepared to make bookings. October saw the Federation staging a second EMGAS demonstration, this time 'Eating for a healthy heart'.

A new venture was an Antiques Day undertaken by Henry Spencer of Retford, and the members also knitted hundreds of vests for the Ethiopian Appeal showing that they were concerned about their less fortunate friends throughout the world, contributing also to the Lesotho and Maldive Appeals.

Executive elections found Caroline Raven. Lois Weedon and Anne Dickens, Moulton Aft as Vice Chairmen, and Beryl Oldrey as Treasurer. We said goodbye to Gill Gray, Long Buckby and Sue Wood, Welford, and welcomed Anne Pooley, Irchester as VCOs. Just to illustrate the breadth of the work of Community and International Affairs, the Panel reported on the Laws of Obscenity and Film Censorship, Social Security, the Death Grant, Reform of Rates, Radioactive Waste, Dog Licences, Drug Abuse, Transfer of Money between Spouses, the Financing of the BBC and the Warnock Report. Surveys continued apace with Hedgerows, Barns and Bats being two of the subjects. For the County Pond Survey we received a Certificate for our contribution to the Council of Europe's Campaign on the Water's Edge in the UK. This was fronted by Ruth Moffat, Boddington.

All other activities continued such as Grow, Gather and Gain at Barnwell Manor, 4-day trip to Ross-on-Wye, outings to London and Salisbury and many sporting ventures. We were also helped by very able members in their own fields, particularly Mrs. Mary Titman,

Ruth Moffat, Boddington – Conservation Project.

Oundle for Bowls. One very sad moment came when Mrs. Maureen Payne, Mears Ashby, who had been Chairman of Sports, died suddenly. She had been instrumental in negotiating with the Sports Council enabling the Federation to take up unusual sports – canoeing, cycling round Rutland Water, Orienteering and Stepping Out Days (Dance and movement).

By this time our membership was 5,866 belonging to 181 WIs, and I had become the Federation's representative on the Farming Wildlife Advisory Group, Rural Voice, the Corby Police Consultative Committee and the Northamptonshire Rural Community Council. Mrs. Cockram was a member of this Council and in later years we both became Chairman, which was a great honour representing also CPRE, CLA, NFU, Northamptonshire Association of Local Councils, Northamptonshire Acre (Action with Communities in Rural England). All these organisations had to agree on any course of action and a Rural Strategy for Northamptonshire was first produced in 1983 developing into a final manifesto in 1987 and a National manifesto for Rural England in the 1991.

I still find myself Chairman in 1986, with the added honour of being appointed to the Public Afffairs sub-committee of the National Federation. This meant being NF representative on the CECG (Consumers in the European Community Group). We had numerous papers to digest and on this particular body we looked at European Directives and said what we felt about re-naming some very well-known British products; also discussing nutritional labelling, pesticides and food additives, etc.

Another by-product of the National committee was to lecture at Denman and I remember a particular debate on farming v. conservation when I had to take on a member who by a strange coincidence had taught my daughters Geography at their school in Guildford and had a double First from Cambridge. Was I nervous!! Not nearly as much as when I was rung up one evening by the Chairman, Anne Stamper, and asked to go to Pebble Mill the next morning to represent National and discuss the lack of cervical cancer screening on The Pamela Armstrong programme with Edwina Currie, MP, and Dr. Youll of the Christie Institute, a well-known cancer hospital in the North. The WI had conducted a survey on this but it was before my time so I spent the whole night researching what I could and set off the next morning for Birmingham in fear and trepidation. No need to worry as I had Edwina to advise me! They tried to keep us apart until the actual programme, but she managed to find out that this

Cottesbrooke Garen Party, 1987 – Anne Dickens, Joyce Haynes, Mildred Cockram, Caroline Raven.

was my first TV appearance and then proceeded to advise me as to what to wear – too late as I did not take any extra clothes with me. Did I not tell you that the WI gives you excellent opportunities to experience all aspects of life?

Back to rural Northamptonshire, thank heavens, and the beautiful setting of Kelmarsh Hall and its garden was the sight that greeted eight cyclists, all suffering to some degree from cerebal palsy, nearly at the end of their 1,000 mile journey though the British Isles raising funds. They and their back-up team were warmly welcomed by Kelmarsh, Harrington and Arthingworth who played host at their stop-over.

The highlight of the year was the Garden Party at Cottesbrooke Hall when we were privileged to have HRH Princess Alice, Duchess of Gloucester with us for the afternoon. The day was bright and sunny and the garden a picture as we watched the 70th Birthday Celebration pageant depicting the WI through the Ages. Nine WIs had rehearsed separately but had come together under the direction of Mary Stober, Flore, to give a splendid performance to two packed houses. Hackle ton & District gave keep-fit demonstrations and were much admired for their precision, elegance and musicality.

Northamptonshire were in the Chair for the East of England Inter-County Show with Anne Dickens Moulton Aft. as designer, the theme being WI Life and Leisure, and we were awarded a Highly Commended Certificate for our marquee. Sports, with chairman Anne Mackley, Weston Favell, became very competitive with Badminton, Golf, Tennis, Bowls, Rounders. Bridge and Scrabble were added as was a Swimming Gala and Self-Defence classes.

Crafts continued with their excellent displays at all events, their newest venture being the wall hanging which was the brain child of Mrs. Josie Crisell, Croughton. This meant every WI producing a cross stitch piece of work depicting their own area, which was eventually made up into the beautiful wall hanging which hangs in WI House. Music were involved with the pageant at Cottesbrooke and also with a Drama Festival when 19 WIs had performed at the Thomas a Becket School in Northampton.

The year ended with the ever popular Christmas Appetiser with carols but this time with a difference as five of these were composed by members for the 1984 competition. They were made up into a booklet at a cost of £1.50 each.

The Council meeting was held in Spinney Hill Hall on 28th October, and in making Education the main topic of my address I welcomed Caroline Raven as the newly appointed Voluntary Education Co-ordinator. Having talked about education, first in our own WIs, then through our Federation, Denman College, and National, I mentioned one newspaper stating that 'if wives were successful their husbands experienced stress, but if they stayed at home leading an inactive life, again the husband or family suffered'. The WI offered a happy compromise. Liz Fox, Barnwell, our newly appointed Treasurer, was welcomed as we said goodbye and thank you to Beryl Oldrey, who had resigned. The appeal for the extension had reached the halfway mark as £10,000 had been raised in the first year and we had started the building work.

Don't put your daughter on the stage, Mrs. Worthington was the request of our speaker Maev Alexander, an accomplished and talented actress. At the end of the meeting all past Federation Chairmen were called on to the platform and in appreciation of the 24 years she had been our Federation Treasurer, Miss Margaret Aspinal was presented with garden furniture, flowers and two specially bound books to which each WI had contributed a page.

A Day of Dance, Fitness and Health was held at Kingsthtorpe Upper School in March 1987 looked after by Nona Pollard, Holcot, the new

Miss Margaret Aspinal with gifts on her retirement in 1986.

Chairman of Sports, whilst Gillian Smith, King's Sutton, took on the responsibility of Community and International Affairs, and organised two events, a Russian Evening and a Cook's Tour of Europe.

It was this year that we introduced the 500 Club as a fund-raising operation, an idea we had picked up from Cambridgeshire when we visited their Annual General Meeting.

As half the monies needed for the extension had kindly been raised by members, we started on the work on 29th April 1987. We held our meetings next door by kind permission of our neighbour, but our first shock came when the builders found not one, but two wells which they knew nothing about when they started to dig the foundations. Although this problem was quickly solved it cost an extra £850. However, by the end of August all was finished and we had a much larger committee room, and Kathleen Pinton's office on the ground floor meant she could work and meet members in much more comfort. The actual cost of the extension was £34,465.48p Ann Denny, Ashby St.

Ledgers, gained first place at the Royal Show in the Huxley Cup. For her floral interpretation of Country Colour she chose Ireland. Another Anne, Anne Dickens was again the designer at the East of England Show and a Highly Commended was achieved for her interpretation of 'The Good Life'.

In September we officially opened the WI House extension and we

Opening of the WI House extension – Agnes Salter, Joyce Haynes and Mildred Cockram.

were delighted to have National Chairman, Agnes Salter with us for the whole day. Many members came to meet and talk to her.

For the Annual Council Meeting at Spinney Hill Hall on 27th November, Sue Arnold gave a talk entitled The Pleasures and Problems of being a Royal Reporter, and A Northamptonshire Picture was launched costing £32.50 each signed by the artist Helen Clayson. £3 from each sale was given to the Federation.

I said my goodbye as Chairman quoting from Arnold Bennett's 'Twenty Four Hours a Day' –

You wake up in the morning and lo! Your purse is magically filled with 24 hours of the unmanufactured tissue of the universe of your life. It is yours. It is the most precious possession. No-one can take it from you. It is unstealable. And no-one received either more or less than you receive. And it is yours to use as you will.

Although I didn't realise it at the time this was virtually similar to one of Miss Simpson's early quotes. Does anything ever change?

Caroline Raven took over the chairmanship in 1988 and the theme for the year was Country Colour, the title of the National WI Visual Arts Project. It was also Northamptonshire's 70th Anniversary so the planned events were an Exhibition, an Edwardian Garden Party, and a Celebration Revue.

Early in the year we held an Open Day at WI House where members' entries for the Country Colour competition were on display – Paintings, Folding Display Panels and Anniversary Posters. This was supplemented by displays of the hobbies of Executive members. Then on 26th March a Health and Beauty Day was held at the Sponne School, Towcester, where members could choose between Healthy Eating, Skincare and Make-up, Stress, Well Woman and Yoga. This event was closely followed by a Calor Gas and Rayburn Cookery Demonstration.

The year was also designated Formation 700 by National when it was hoped this extra number of WIs would be opened throughout the country.

In the middle of April we took over the Abington Museum with our superb exhibition of the History of 70 years in Northamptonshire, when 1,200 visited on the opening day on the Monday with comparable numbers each day ending with 500 on the Sunday. Anne Dickens, Moulton Aft., Pauline Duff, Brixworth, Jane Stonebridge, Cranford, and Joan White, Weston Favell Aft., were responsible for the collection and staging of the WI memorabilia.

Caroline Raven, second left, with Mildred Cockram, Nancy Walker, Joan Chester and Anne Dickens. Planting a tree in Becketts Park to celebrate the 70th Anniversary.

At the end of this month the grand performance of the Celebration Revue was held at Spinney Hill Hall, Northampton, with groups selected from all other the county.

In May Grow, Gather and Gain went to Pitsford, and then on to the Edwardian Garden Party at Lamport Hall in June. As well as stalls depicting the era there was a Youth Band playing, Dancing, a Costume parade and competition, and singing by Whittlebury Choir.

A Celebration Fashion Show staged by Clive Cavanagh in

September was a sell-out and in between these major events the usual Bowls, Table Tennis, Rounders, Scrabble, Netball, and outings to London, Norwich, the Lake District and the Black Country Museum. Sports found us having an inter-county competition with a Gloucestershire WI, Taynton and Tiberton. A minibus was hired for the day with Nona Pollard as driver.

The Annual Meeting on 25th October featured Pauline Brown, Principal of Denman College, who brought the great news that Denman had been saved by members raising the required one million pounds. She was followed by Monty Moss with his amusing talk '130 years of Moss Bros.' Goodbyes were said to Liz Fox, Barnwell, and Marie Percival, Hunsbury Hill from Executive. Marie had excelled at table tennis and had represented Northamptonshire nationally, being runner-up with Wendy Steers, Gayton, in 1988, when they had received £30 which enabled the Sports committee to lay on special coaching the following year. This year we also said goodbye to Beryl Eady, Moulton Aft. who had done so much reporting activities of the WI in both *Northants and Bedfordshire Life*, as well as helping with Round-up and other publicity.

This year, because of the postal strike, a county distribution of the newsletter had been devised by the Editor, which saved the Federation approximately £1,300 per month. This meant me travelling throughout the county each month delivering to Group Conveners who kindly delivered to their areas. Some of those original helpers are still delivering to-day. In 1987 the 500 Club had been introduced a few years previously and county raffles had been held in alternate years to National.

The sad news at the beginning of 1989 was that National Chairman, Agnes Salter, had died. Her great love had been WI Markets. A Denman College Travel Fund was set up in her name to enable members from far flung counties to obtain bursaries to help with their travel.

Themes for the year had become established by now in Northamptonshire and 1989 was to be Food and Farming Year. The Steering Committee for this had been set up in 1986 and I attended all the meetings until Caroline took over in 1988.

Our first event this year was a Caribbean Evening at the Guildhall on 30th March, followed by the Spring in Bloom Produce Show at Moulton College on 15th April. This month finished with a demonstration of Four Seasons of Food and Flowers.

The main event of the Year was the Food and Farming Fairs when

Caroline toured the county with a sponsored and chauffeured Land Rover visiting WIs to give support to their events. to celebrate this year. Half the proceeds would be staying with WI and the County would gratefully receive the other half.

In May Grow, Gather and Gain was held in the Apricot village of Aynho and late in June a very entertaining Old Tyme Music Hall was held at the Royal Theatre, Northampton.

A Fitness and Dance Day, on 23rd September at Kingsthorpe Upper School, saw many members trying to keep fit, whilst others travelled to Bruges, or to York, or entered the National Choir Singing Festival. We also started the now extremely popular Literary Luncheons and our first guest was Angela Huth, who had written many novels and was at one time a photo journalist on the *Sunday Express*. These events were catered for by our own county Catering committee and so many talented cooks have headed this committee since Mrs. Monicreff Dickens in the early days. Starting with Audrey Carter, Gt. Doddington, there has been Heather Jeffries, Naseby, Angela Farrington, Hargrave, Winnie Shurville, Weston Favell, Diana Birch, Yelvertoft, Judy Ayton, Greens Norton and Carolyn Libby, Everdon.

At the Council Meeting, on 24th October at Spinney Hill Hall, Mrs. Raven talked about the new Constitution which would be discussed in 1990, about the fire that had occurred at WI House in April when someone had broken a window and thrown something burning into the general office. All hands on deck again and it was business as usual in a short space of time.

At this time Winnie Shurville had been appointed County Treasurer, whilst in line with other former members Suzanne May (nee Palfreyman) had become National Treasurer. She had been National's representative on Transport 2000 as she lived in London and used public transport a great deal and it was for her work on this organisation that she was eventually awarded the OBE.

Janet Cannetty-Clarke, an accomplished pianist, musician, lecturer, conductor and WI member for 25 years gave a delightful recital of music and anecdotes. Her 'Interlude with Music' was described as 'just magic'. A Nosegay Competition was won by Bugbrooke WI with Irchester second.

The Travel committee under the chairmanship of Anthea Butler, Geddington & Newton, took members to Lincoln. Westonbirt, Bruges and London and the year ended with a Swimming Gala for all the family at the Cripps Centre, Norhampton General Hospital on 25th November.

Chapter 9
REVISED CONSTITUTION AND A NEW CENTURY
1990–2004

The theme for 1990 was to be Forward to the Future.

The dominant topic of this year was to be the revision of the Constitution. It was stated that our Constitution and Rules had survived the test of time but they urgently needed revising, updating and bringing into line with current legal requirements. This would allow for the protection of the Companies Act to provide a practical and protective net when need arose.

National headquarters were moving into new premises in New Kings Road in Fulham which they were buying instead of renting as in the past. 39 Eccleston Street and 63 Chester Street had been their home since 1926. Anne Ballard took early retirement this year as NF General Secretary having served for 21 years. Sadly it was reported that Miss Meriel Withall MBE, who had been variously assistant and secretary from 1936 to 1972, with a break of five years in between, had died.

12th February, saw Ken Hom giving one of his superb Chinese Cookery demonstrations at Spinney Hill Hall, and although his staff found time to eat food prepared by the catering committee, he never stopped long enough to take more than a drink of mineral water. A County Exhibition of Crafts was held from which selected items would go forward to the National Exhibition at Rufford, Nottinghamshire.

As it was National's 75th Anniversary, HM the Queen, honoured members with a visit to the AGM at the Royal Albert Hall, and this was also when the revised Constitution was first voted on, the most important reason for this being financial. Under the previous Constitution NFWI lost out on investments because of time restrictions in transferring documents and members of Executive living out of London. In addition their liability as managing trustees was unlimited. And although it was unlikely that any member would be called upon to put in personal money, there was always a risk that they would be asked to do so. The various resolutions were passed and it was left to

HM the Queen at the 75th Anniversary AGM, 1990.

Federations to decide whether they, too, wished to become Companies Limited by Guarantee.

An Old Tyme Music Hall was held at the Royal Theatre in June, and what a lively and entertaining evening this was.

Bodnant Gardens was the destination in June, followed by Shugborough, Eastbourne and Norfolk. But the highlight of the year was a trip to Canada to see the birthplace of the WI in Stoney Creek, Ontario. One member recalled the brilliant colour of the leaves in the Fall, the beautiful Parliament buildings in Ottawa, black squirrels everywhere, elegant Georgian style houses in Kingston, the dizzy heights of the CN tower in Toronto, the awe-inspiring sight and sound of Niagara Falls, and of course the visit to the Adelaide Hunter Hoodless homestead. Sporty members joined in an Inter-County

Sports Day with Bedfordshire, Berkshire, Derbyshire, Gloucestershire and Warwickshire. This was a lovely fun day, and it was announced nationally that we were in the East Midlands Group and as I was Sports chairman at this time, together with Diana Benarr, Redwell, vice-chairman, we spent many happy hours travelling to Newark for these quarterly meetings.

On 11th September we took over the Pavilion at the Northampton Cricket Ground for tea parties to celebrate National's 75th Anniversary. £10,000 sponsorship had been received by National from Tetleys, together with gifts for each WI to help towards their events. The charities to benefit were Barnardos to provide holidays for disadvantaged children in SE England, the Cancer/Leukaemia ward at Birmingham General Hospital, the Camphill Village Trust for mentally handicapped children in Wales and the South West and the British Association for the Deaf in the North of England. Northamptonshire sent £9,000 as its contribution collected from WIs. Nationally members collected £401,162.

30th October saw members at the Annual Council Meeting when Mrs. Kathleen Pinton, retiring Federation Secretary was presented with cheque for £1,000 which had been contributed to by members. She was to be succeeded by Mrs. Anne Pooley, Irchester, who was also a VCO. This meeting saw the launch of the Northamptonshire Village Book.

The main speaker was Mr.

Katheen Pinton, Federation Secretary.

Anne Pooley, Federation Secretary 1991, with Gunilla Loe and Teresa Carr.

David Shepherd, Landscape and Wildlife artist who talked about his great concern for the many endangered species, and the setting up of his own Conservation Foundation in 1987, thus repaying the debt he said he owed to the animals he painted and which had brought him much success.

The subscription was raised to £7.50, still a far cry from the onetenth of an agricultural wage which was the rate agreed when the first

WI opened. Most of National's financial worries would have been solved if this rate had been maintained.

In November British Gas again provided an evening of cookery, this time with Christmas entertaining in mind.

A visit to Harwell on 5th December was followed by a Celebration of Christmas on the 7th under the direction of Mr. Malcolm Tyler, County Music Adviser.

The Regional Round of the WI Driver of the Year was held in Nottingham and of our three representatives June Elias, Stanion, was the overall winner and would go on to the National Finals at Donnington Park.

Two more surveys were undertaken by members – Village Greens and Hedgehogs, and the Community and International Affairs committee, now under the chairmanship of Gillian Smith, King's Sutton, organised a Countryside Day at Irchester, a visit to an ACWW Awareness Day in Oxfordshire, and Footpath Walks followed by a meeting with the County Footpath Officers who were available to answer and discuss all aspecs of these expeditions.

Into 1991 with Federation Chairman Winnie Shurville, Weston Favell, vice-chairmen Sue Bird, Easton & Collyweston and Christine Farmer, Preston Capes and Malvina Keech, Cranford, Treasurer. Sadly some members had said goodbye – Valerie McWilliam, Thornby, on moving to Scotland, Anne Dickens, Moulton Aft. and Marian Barker, Mears Ashby. But with the advent of the new Constitution the office of President no longer existed and so we were losing Mrs. Mildred Cockram. She would be sadly missed for her dedication to the WI; she had been a wonderful ambassador, and a staunch and loyal supporter of the Federation and its members and had probably visited nearly every WI in her time as member, County Chairman and County President. She was presented with various gifts and a cheque for a commemmorative item for WI House, as well as the Federation President's badge she had worn with pride for over 20 years.

The Welcome to the USA evening at Sulgrave Manor was organised in June when we were treated to delicious American snacks, the lively music of a jazz band, and square dancing. In October Mrs. Ursula Goh, Chairman of Projects ACWW was a charming speaker at our International evening Where in the World is the WI? Earlier this year saw the launch of our first ACWW project to raise money to help build four classrooms for Pre and Primary education in Nepal. This was at the instigation of Mrs. Anne Wright, Wappenham, later to be followed by more projects initiated by Mrs. Susan Addams, Welton.

Winnie Shurville, County Chairman 1990.

The first Triennial meeting was held at the NEC, Birmingham; this was a two-day meeting with a concert at the end of the first meeting, when two choirs from Northamptonshire joined those from other counties. They were from Whittlebury and Yelvertoft. This Triennial is another update of the Constitution requiring National to meet with delegates from WIs every three years. Mrs. Shurville outlined the streamlining of various sub-committees and Mrs. Malvina Keech explained the resolution which would made Northamptonshire a Company limited by guarantee.

As the Federation owned its own property and had considerable financial assets and employed staff, without this change Executive would be liable as individuals in the event of any claim against the Federation exceeding its assets. In future it would mean all these members would only be liable to the extent of £1 each. The resolution was passed unanimously.

At the end of the meeting we spent 45 minutes in the world of Noel Coward with Judith Baxter and David Mackie singing both his well-known and not so well-known music and songs. We had been successful in obtaining sponsorship for a new demonstration kitchen at the top of WI House, and to complete the project, Anne Dickens, Diana Benarr and myself decorated both the kitchen and members' room.

Outings were a two-day tour to Suffolk, taking in Constable, Sizewell and Girton -what a heady mixture! A holiday to Amsterdam was another feature, with further outings to Derby, Calke Abbey, Cambridge and Anglesey Abbey. The grand finale to the year was the pantomime Sleeping Beauty at Lings Theatre, Weston Favell, with a good attendance at all three performances. This was under the direction of Susan Burman, Mears Ashby with Anne Dickens chairman.

An Antiques Road Show on 27th February took place at the

beginning of 1992. This was held at the Old Barn, Hunsbury Hill, always a delightful venue for a meeting.

A Spring into Summer Day at Sponne School, Towcester, saw members getting into shape with Yoga, Make up and Beauty Care together with Healthy Eating. A Village Scrapbook competition was launched on 1st April to continue until 31st March 1993 to record a social history of the community, a request from the principal Archivist at the County Records Office.

To emphasise healthy eating, The Eating to Live or Living to Eat conference organised by Kellogs at Daventry Community Centre was educational and enjoyable. Crochet, calligraphy and decoupage were the requests for classes from members to the new Combined Crafts committee. These continued together with the Down Your Way requests to take various classes and demonstrations to different areas of the county. Christina Sergeant, Kelmarsh, Harrington & Arthingworth was the new chairman of this committee. She was a talented flower arranger. Another new chairman, Marian Barker, Mears Ashby, took up the reins of the much reduced Home Economics committee, who were responsible for Grow, Gather and Gain at Sywell Country Park, and a Fun with Dyeing Day at Barnwell.

Pam Farrington, Potterspury, and Shirley Robinson, Boddington joined the ranks of VCOs and Croquet, Archery and a Treasure Hunt were added to the Sports itinerary.

28th October, 1992, found chairman, Winnie Shurville at the Annual Council Meeting congratulating the new treasurer, Malvina Keech, Cranford who had succeeded in successfully transferring all the Federation accounts to the computer. A new era had dawned and new skills had to be learnt. The theme of Lot's to Do in '92 had proved to be prophetic. There had been Grow, Gather and Gain at Sywell Country Park, two Wine, Words and Music events at Rushton and Brackley, outings to Stirling, Hampton Court, a Federation visit to Denman College, all the usual sports events and the annual appearances at the East of England and Abington Shows.

Mrs. Anne Wright, Wappenham, always a stalwart supporter of ACWW, attended the 21st Triennial Conference in The Hague, Holland, as our representative.

Within Living Memory was launched at the Council meeting, and the speaker, Mr. Ian Redmond took us into the world of mountain gorillas with slides and sounds.

1993 was the Federation's 75th Anniversary and our main celebraion was the weekend at Pitsford with Radio Northampton and all the activities associated with a WI event – exhibits, stalls, crafts fair, refreshments, children's fun and games, with Celebrity Cricket on the Sunday with teams from Anglia and Central Television. Admission was £4, £1 for children.

Music & Drama organised their choral celebration, Captain Noah and his Floating Zoo; Home Economics master-minded another Grow, Gather & Gain, this time at Naseby, and also ran a series of mouth-watering Party Times around the county tempting palates and challenging waistlines.

Travel transported a good many members to a number of places – Sudeley Castle, RHS Wisley and Harrogate to name a few. Always of course they provided coaches for the East of England Show, the National AGM and our own Council Meeting.

Our speaker at this meeting at Spinney Hill Hall on 1st November, 1993 was Rosemary Hawthorne, whose husband was the Vicar of Tetbury. She was a former professional actress, and although they had seven children she still found time to collect, lecture and write about fashion history Her talk was A Brief History of Unmentionables and the biggest laugh of the evening came when she produced bottle green school knickers complete with pocket. How many of us must have remembered those garments, albeit in different equally drab colours!

Over five days in June members had walked the Anniversary Walk throughout the county starting with Kelmarsh in the North, down to Farthingstone in the south and then back up again to WI House in Northampton.

This year saw the renovation of the Denman bedroom for which members had raised the sum of £1,795.65. We had been given a bed by a kind sponsor.

1993 had found us with chairman Sue Bird, Easton & Collyweston and treasurer, Sue Tait, Cottesbrooke, and Carolyn Libby, Everdon, was the latest VCO to be appointed.

One of the last events of the year was the Gala Evening at Spinney Hill Hall when Janet Canetty-Clark had played a selection of works for the piano. An Operatic Society and a Youth Brass Band completed the line up of performers and so we moved on to the next year.

At the beginning of 1994 the first County Choir was established, and their first performance was much later in the year in December at the Christmas Appetiser in St. Michael's Church, Northampton. Their conductor at that time was Mrs. Marilyn Woodrow.

Sue Bird, chairman, with County Banner in background.

It was decided at this time to disband Groups. They had never been part of the Constitution and had caused a great deal of extra work to the County Treasurer, dealing with all the monies involved, and there was always the problem of finding Conveners. So we took meetings around the county telling them of our idea to divide the county into Areas. There would be 15 instead of the 33 Groups. There would be an Area Organiser and an Assistant and all events would be self-supporting. Classes, etc. to be arranged within these Areas, with the tutors possibly coming from within the Area also as there was felt to be so much latent expertise. There would be one large social meeting a year. It was felt these meetings would attract new members, that it would facilitate opportunities for learning and recreation within easy reach at reasonable cost, and would also raise the level of interest and pleasure obtained from WI membership.

Grow, Gather and Gain took place at Everdon in May and Travel organised outings to the Birmingham Jewellery Centre, Exbury Gardens and Snowdonia/Anglesey and Chester. The birthplace of the first WI at Llanfair PG proved a great attraction. An outing was made to Greenwich where the Fan Museum was visited.

Crafts committee offered Smocking, Rag Rugs and Wallhanging to members, which by this time numbered 4,722 from 153 WIs. Nationally there were 293,700 members.

The second Triennial meeting was held at the NEC, Birmingham in June when Michael Palin was the speaker. This was held over two days and Northampton members decided on the second day to wear hats as their had been so few on the first day. We had obviously turned back the clock but it was something members enjoyed if the number of comments received were to be believed.

On 2nd and 9th June Play Days were held at the Royal Theatre in Northampton, when members were split into three groups, one to visit the extensive wardrobe, one to meet the Director, and the other to have a tour of this enchanting Victorian theatre. A matinee performance of Charley's Aunt was the icing on the cake.

Back to Northampton and to our own Council Meeting when David Battie of Antiques Roadshow fame was the speaker. We learnt that Pam Farrington, Potterspury, had been successful in her long distance walk across Scotland and had raised a great deal of money for the Federation on walking this 212 miles.

A very special meeting was the inaugural lecture in memory of Sir Richard Livingstone held in the Oxford Examination Schools and presented by Richard Smethurst, Provost of Worcester College. His lecture called Sesame and Lilies featured the importance of adult education and the ways in which we can influence those around us. I was particularly delighted to be asked to attend to represent the county as an old friend of mine from Surrey, Elizabeth Southey was in the chair as National Chairman.

1994 ended with five meetings to discuss the hidden dangers of Radon. Members attending were asked to do a simple experiment and findings would be published in due course.

As was the practice at the beginning of every year, the VCOs organised information meetings for all WI members, be they Presidents, Secretaries, Treasurers, would be committee members, Public speaking days, etc. and these usually took place over several weeks in different parts of the county. Weird and wonderful titles were thought up to encourage members to attend, and taking them as a whole much valuable information was exchanged and members really did enjoy meeting those from other WIs to talk about their similarities or their differences, at the same time gaining new ideas to take back to their meetings.

A Fashion Show by Mary Robinson of Higham Ferrers took place at Spinney Hill Hall on 6th April. This advertised fashion for all ages and sizes, in casual, day and evening wear. Home Economics organised Picnic Times where members learnt how to prepare tasty food for the future under the title Looking Ahead to Spring. Venues were Paulerspury, Brigstock, Barby and Yardley Hastings.

The Intermediate General Meeting found Northamptonshire members travelling to Blackpool, and being accommodated at the Burnley Friendly Hotel on the night before as it was too far to travel there and back in one day. As accommodation was limited most members had to share double rooms, and this certainly led to a friendly introduction to other WI members. Very rarely did members fall out, because VCOs and staff knew everyone so well we were able to put compatible members together.

Grow, Gather and Gain went to Braunston and there were outings to Bath, Hay on Wye and Hereford, and a 4-day holiday to Devon, staying in Plymouth.

A special meeting was convened to discuss many county matters, such as the new areas, the newsletter, federation committees, etc., in other words to discuss the future of the WI which was chaired by Sue Bird. The main concern was that we were showing a deficit of £15,000 and although members enjoyed events when they did attend, fewer were doing so. This left us with two options, either to greatly reduce our expenditure or to generate a much larger income. The role of the county was to encourage links between WI members to lead to greater participation. This is why Areas were introduced, but as with most new ideas this was slow to get off the ground and members still did not attend in any great numbers. The questionnaire that had been sent out showed that only about 50% had attended a county event in the last twelve months, so it was time for a radical re-think of the type of event organised. Committee members could be reduced to save expenses and this was in the pipeline. The Northamptonshire WI News was a valuable form of communication and in fact did contribute to funds. Members did not, however, object to more advertising which would lead to additional revenue. This would also be the last year

The Northampton Show.

Northamptonshire served on the East of England Inter-County Show committee as it was felt too difficult to continue to find the personnel to contribute to both this Show and the Northampton Show, occurring so quickly one after the other and with the complication that the latter was in holiday time. 20 years of participating was probably a good contribution, but the WIs in the north of the county would no doubt miss Northamptonshire's presence.

The Annual Council meeting on 26th October had Deric Longden as it speaker with the subject Laughter and Tears. After this meeting we found ourselves with Sue Tait, Cottesbrooke, as chairman and Diana Benarr, Redwell and Sue Lineham, Yardley Gobion were the vice- chairman. Reta Evans, Aston-le-Walls & Appletree was the new treasurer.

The end of the year brought sadness when it was learnt that Christine Sutton had died. Her beloved Sports committee had organised a Treasure Hunt based around Pitsford and finishing with refreshment at Mears Ashby.

Members visited Wedgewood and Bridgemere Gardens where they could see the WI Garden which had gained a medal at the Chelsea Flower Show; also Hereford and the Cider Museum. The year ended with Christmas at the Castle, Wellingborough – demonstrations of

Food and Flowers which whetted everyone's appetite for the coming festivities, as did the Christmas Appetiser with its songs, readings and carols in early December.

We began 1996 with a Romania Day at WI House when Susan Addams told members about her visit and we learnt about the goods that could be donated to the Filiast Orphanage in the south- west of the country.

In March we were transported to another, South Africa, an area of vast contrasts and this evening at Guilsborough School provided members with a glimpse of some of the countries that are part of this great continent.

After Easter the destination was Lacock Abbey and Chippenham in Wiltshire to visit the Fox Talbot Photography Museum, but more romantically two coach loads of members ventured to Paris for this springtime excursion. We crossed the channel for the first time via Le Shuttle, which took just 35 minutes – what a feat of engineering! We had a three night stay and were able to visit the Eiffel Tower, Versailles and Chantilly.

The Intermediate General Meeting was at Cardiff in June and we travelled down to stay at a nearby hotel overnight. Always on these expeditions we made arrangements to have a meal at a WI on the way back.

Fishing is listed as the most popular sport in this country and so to keep up with current trends we organised a Fly Fishing Taster Evening at Ravensthorpe Reservoir. This was an evening event and members were asked to wear a hat and sunglasses and to take along wet weather gear – just in case. Darts and Skittles, together with Bowls, indoor and out, continued to be popular, as was Scrabble.

The County Lunch at Byfield had Lyndsay Hacket-Pain, ACWW Treasurer, talking to members, whilst the County Produce Show at Rothwell had the theme Autumn Glory with three main categories, Flowers, Crafts and Cookery.

Members were encouraged to enter the Planter competition for the Evening with Bob Flowerdew at the Billing Garden Centre and Miniature Furniture was demonstrated by Geoff Daniel who had taken lecture tours on the QE2.

The Annual Council Meeting had Jenni Murray of Woman's Hour as its speaker. She gave some delightful and some rather sad insights into the lot of women during 50 years, making us all appreciate what a better life we had now, and if truth be know how much the WI had contributed to this over these years.

Short Mat Bowls winners, Blisworth – Jean Tufnell, Bobbie Nelson, Jean Wells and Dorothy Rigby.

The Memorial Book was launched at this meeting to perpetuate the memories of loyal and loved members who had passed away. WIs could give a small donation in their memory and this would provide a bursary to attend an educational course.

A competition was also launched for a new WI Badge and the eventual winner was a member of Bugbrooke WI.

Walks were continued during most months of the year, either individually by WIs, or as a county initiative. These were all listed under The Great Outdoors and had a qualified leader to take members around the area chosen. Sport & Leisure were responsible for these excursions, and the Leader of the team at this time was Sue Richards, Cosgrove, suggesting that her team covered everything from walking to skydiving. Just get in touch and they would organise it!

Agenda 21 – winners Village Map Competition. Barby – Hazel Parsons.

1997 saw Sue Tait, Cottesbrooke still in office as Chairman with vice-chairmen Christine Farmer and Malvina Keech. Reta Evans continued as treasurer. Sadly this year we heard that a former chairman, Nancy Walker, had died.

The County Lunch was held at Barnwell in March, when Colin Tarn, a former musical director of the Mermaid Theatre, was the speaker. He had written and produced the Denman Fanfare performed at the College in 1995.

Talking of food we then went to Milton Malsor later in the month when we were given information so that we could make informed decisions on what we should be buying in the future and the ethical issues involved. Genetic engineering was top of the agenda. Meanwhile WIs were busy producing Village Maps as a local indicator of what is really impotant and what could be changed for the better. This linked up with Agenda 21, a programme of action for the 21st century signed by world leaders in Rio in 1992 and aimed at producing local responses to global problems such as depletion of natural resources and the growing amount of waste. These Village Maps would highlight those

Henry Sandon with Malvina Keech and Sue Tait, Chairman.

things worth preserving to pass on to future generations. As well as Grow, Gather and Gain, which went to Stoke Bruerne, a memorable afternoon at Daventry with Henry Sandon of Antiques Roadshow fame, with his love of Worcester porcelain, was a special coup. He was not only accompanied by his wife but brought along his delightful little poodle Snowy. Afternoon tea was also provided, all for the sum of £10. A four-day trip to Northumbria and Durham in the Autumn provided a welcome break for many members. Hexham, Alnwick Castle, Kielder Water and the Beamish Museum were amongst the attractions visited, whereas in August Royal Brierley Crystal and the Broadfield Glass Musem were our points of call. Another interesting destination was Colchester and the Beth Chatto Gardens. I have often wondered how

Wickstead Park, 1986 – WI Markets members with Des Barnes.

the Travel team kept thinking up these wonderful trips. They seem to have exhausted every possible avenue.

More advertisements in the newsletter had been sanctioned by members for the newsletter, and these together with a more colourful format helped to make this publication much more attractive.

The Annual Council Meeting on 30th October was when members heard from Bill Giles, the BBC weatherman, and the national Triennial Meeting had Jonathan Porritt of Friends of the Earth telling us that we should avoid the 'doom and gloom' mentality and think positively about sustainable development. Barby were the winners of the Village Map competition, but all entries were to be displayed at the County Records Office.

The *Evening Telegraph* invited us to Wickstead Park to celebrate their 100 years, and we were delighted when Des Barnes of *Coronation Street* visited our stand.

New beginnings were in sight for our 80th birthday in 1988, as many members were leaving Executive – Sue Tait, Pauline Duff, Caroline Raven and Winnie Shurville. Our new chairman was Christine Farmer, with Malvina Keech vice-chairman.

Another stalwart we were going to miss was our secretary Anne Pooley, who had undertaken this post for the past eight years, quite an achievement She was eventually succeeded by Margaret Foster, who at that time was not a member but later joined Cranford.

At this time we still had seven Markets in the county and members are being urged to support them: Brackley, Daventry, Kettering, Northampton, Oundle, Towcester and Wellingborough By now teams of members had been appointed to replace sub-committee members, resulting in halving the number involved in county work, at the same time removing contact with approximately 50 WIs. Time would tell if this was the right strategy but at that time making ends meet was the priority.

The Cooking Canon, i.e. John Eley came to the Castle, Wellingborough to demonstrate food for Easter, whilst Michael Bowyer, National Demonstrator produced exquisite flower arrangements. At this event another Northamptonshire book – *A Century of Village Life* – was launched. This required members to provide photographs of two eras, pre 1925 with the same spot being photographed post 1955. A short text had to accompany these impressions.

The 80th Birthday Revue was held at Thomas a Becket School, Northampton from 17/18th April with a great variety of acts, from line dancing to belly dancing, songs from yesteryear, including wartime favourites to the Music and Drama members performing Oh what a Birthday, was a great entertainment.

Into June with members travelling to Brighton for the Intermediate General Meeting, followed by Aspects of the Sun, a mini-lecture programme consisting of solar buildings, the effect of global warming, sun and skin cancer and genetic engineering for plants to survive the sun. Organised by Meg Mayhew, Yelvertoft, this was held at Brackley and members could

Gt. & Lt. Oakley 70th birthday cake.

1998 Celebration Service, with the Lord Bishop of Peterborough. Federation Chairman, Christine Farmer, second left.

choose which lectures they wished to attend. Talking of Brackley this is when Anne Seckington was appointed a VCO. There were to be three more major events this year starting with the Annual Council Meeting on 22nd October at Spinney Hill Hall when Norman Croucher OBE was the main speaker, then the Civic Service and Reception on 1st November. Finally the Tree Planting Day at Brixworth Country Park. The Civic Service was a memorable Thanksgiving occasion. An anthem with music composed especially by Malcolm Tyler with words by Susan Burman, Mears Ashby set the scene for a very WI service. The Lord Bishop of Peterborough and the High Sheriff of Northamptonshire both attended as did many other dignitaries, and after the service, with bells ringing in triumph they all walked through the late afternoon sunshine to the Guildhall for a splendid tea. At this service Christine Farmer, chairman, reminded everyone of the WI aims and objects:

> The WI is based on the spiritual ideals of fellowship, truth, tolerance and justice. It is a social and educational organisation

Planting of trees – Brixworth Country Park.

offering women the opportunity for friendship and of working and learning together to improve the quality of life in Community and to enable development of individual skills and talent. It exists to give all women the opportunity of working together through the WI Organisation and of putting into practice those ideals for which it stands. In Northamptonshire as members of this large national WI family with over one-quarter of a million members, we are all aware of our declared intent to be to-day's women working for tomorrow's world.

This was followed by the Tree Planting on the 7th, a day again blessed with good weather. WIs had donated various sums to plant their trees. The Park wished to have mainly small trees so where there was a surplus donation this was put to planting the 50 oak trees in the WI Circle, which would channel the views from the main footpath across Pitsford Water – an extremely important part of the future landscape. The small trees planted in the WI coppice would create woodlands that were rich in wildlife value, particularly for flowering plants, birds and invertebrates, thus allowing species that have difficulty in colonising new areas to be able to survive.

Visit to the European Parliament – Kathleen Pinton and Susan Addams with Angela Billingham MEP.

Another highlight which cannot be omitted was the trip to Strasbourg and the European Parliament where we met with our MEP Angela Billingham. So much was learnt on this trip, from how the Parliament is run, what its responsibilities are, etc. The Cathedral at Reims and a tour of the champagne area were also on the agenda – a good time was had by all.

There are so many wonderful and interesting people who have worked tirelessly for the WI in Northamptonshire and two of these were Mary Smeathers of Duston and Ida Twemlow of Welford, both of whom took a great interest in ACWW. You could be fairly sure you would run into either one or both of them at most events. Sadly we have to report their passing, together with Mary Canning, Gretton and Eva Gothard, Nether Heyford.

However, on a happier note we have a newly appointed VCO, Meg Mayhew, Yelvertoft. Christine Farmer remained chairman in 1999, with a new treasurer, Maureen Walton, The Bramptons. The first event of the year was at Spinney Hill Hall with Patrick Anthony calling his demonstration The Reluctant Cook, followed two weeks later by the

County Lunch at Kilsby where Norman Willis, former Chairman of the TUC talked about his love of embroidery whilst typically wandering off the point and talking about the people he had known and the places he had visited.

A Regional Choir Festival took place at Rugby in 14th March when Weldon's String of Pearls was the county's representative and performed to a very high standard.

In June at the Intermediate General Meeting at the Royal Albert Hall we were looking ahead to the Millennium, Northamptonshire having set up it own Millennium ad hoc committee to plan forthcoming events.

Visits were made to the London Museum in April followed by a trip to Wells and Cheddar, and in May members went to Worcester to see the Porcelain Factory and Museum. A 4-day trip over the North Sea to Ireland was the next venture and in July St. Albans and the National Rose Society Garden was the destination. More mundanely members visited a Leaf Farm and a Water Treatment centre later in the year. There was a nucleus of regular travellers who became very good friends over time.

In September the County Lunch at Wilbarston had Jack Darrah speaking on Churchill memorabilia which was housed in the wartime code breaking establishment at Bletchley Park. Music is to the fore again this month with a Choir Learning Day when singers learnt 'The Burning Bush' with Muriel Wallis as conductor at Potterspury followed by an evening Concert. What an exhausting day that must have been.

The Annual Council Meeting at Spinney Hill Hall in October had Hugh de la Hey Davies, former Police Surgeon as its speaker, and at this meeting a resolution reducing the period of service on Executive from three to two years was passed.

As to personalities, Sue Bird, former chairman had been awarded a BA in Cultural Studies, some achievement being a mature student.

Doreen Chown had resigned from the Newsletter team where she had been instrumental in obtaining advertisements for the fifteen years of its existence. I, too, came to the end of my editorship and passed the responsibility to the very capable Diana Birch who was definitely into computers.

The beginning of the large scale County Quiz which reflected the competitive nature of WIs, with teams from most of them taking part, took place at Wickstead Park, and continues to this day, members still competing for the Haynes Cup.

The Millennium is with us and no dire happenings as predicted, and so the year is started with Wine and Cheese evenings in Towcester and Redwell, north and south of the county, with Presidents and three other members joining Executive for a party.

Our second means of celebrating was to have Millennium Boundary Walks throughout the year, covering Northamptonshire's borders with Leicestershire, Bedfordshire, Buckinghamshire, Cambridgeshire and Oxfordshire with members being asked to record their personal mileage.

The Triennial General Meeting at the Wembley Arena made headline news. We stayed overnight at a hotel in Watford as it was too far to travel the length of Northamptonshire picking up delegates and to go there and back in one day. Why did we make the headlines? Because Tony Blair was the

Sundial Project – Welford's Millennium Sundial.

2000 – National AGM with the main speaker, Prime Minister Tony Blair.

Margaret Foster, Federation Secretary, at a Denman College weekend with Jenny Hayes, Anne Mackley and Mary Jackson.

main speaker and misjudged his audience. Instead of promoting ourselves as A Modern Voice for Women, one daily newspaper stated we should stand for Jam, Jerusalem and Attitude. The National Chairman at this time was Helen Carey, Cheshire.

Being Denman Representative has always been one of the most coveted roles one can be asked to undertake, and we have had some excellent ones – Pat Kutas, Milton Malsor, Marion Barker, Mears Ashby, Carolyn Libby, Everdon and last but not least Christine Farmer, Preston Capes. We have always felt very attached to Denman, perhaps because of its early ties with the Elwes family, and possibly because it is not too far for our members to travel to attend, and so we have had Denman Days, Demonstrations, and Denman Weekends galore. This year's weekend in June was followed by a 5-day Scottish holiday, and outings to Windsor and the Earth Centre in Doncaster in July.

A Celebration county picnic was held at Brixworth Country Park in August, starting at the Denman Wood, which was the circle of oak and ash trees planted two years earlier by members. The weather was perfect for pond dipping, an insect safari, a treasure hunt, a guided walk and welly wanging, a competition won by Byron Orme, my grandson.

Members were taken to London to see the Millennium Dome, followed by a river trip. The speaker at the Annual Council Meeting in October was Richard Whiteley of Countdown fame. A new Challenge Trophy was launched with each sub-committee in turn producing a relevant challenge to members. This year Membership asked for Posters, WI Programmes, Press Releases and Covers for the Reference Books which had been sent out to all WIs. The eventual winners were Easton & Collyweston, with Preston Capes second and Geddington & Newton third. Two members of Executive had attended an Extraordinary General Meeting of the National Federation at which it was agreed that the name Board of Trustees would replace Executive Committees, tha the number of members serving on this Board should be reduced to 21 instead of 15 and that the name WI Adviser should replace Voluntary County Organiser.

The year ended with a Christmas Market holiday to Cologne, where members stayed at a hotel in Liege. The Christmas Appetiser always brought members a step closer to celebrating this festival, and all agreed this had been a splendid year. The county calendar which feature cross- stitch had been a sell-out, and members had collected aluminium cans for Alcan resulting in welcome funds being raised. As appropriate in this auspicious year at last the county was on the Internet. We had become a Federation and not a County, but sadly had lost one of our most dedicated members, Joan Bott of Cold Ashby, one of the smallest of our family of WIs.

The first year of the new millennium found Malvina Keech still feeling the new girl in charge when she was elected chairman. Her vice-chairmen were Rosemary Partridge, Ravensthorpe and Reta Evans, Aston-le-Walls & Appletee with Maureen Walton, The Bramptons, continuing as treasurer. Members new to Executive were Gunilla Loe, Harpole, Judy Ayton, Greens Norton and Mary Sheldon, Moulton Aft. The committee structure was altered and so we have fewer of them with Combined Interests, Membership and Travel. The events seemed just as numerous so the year started with Poetry and Pot Luck at Geddington with members being invited to banish the winter blues with amusing and thoughtful poetry. And soup, etc. would follow to help refresh everyone. Then on to an evening at Kislingbury to learn about Japanese traditions with ladies from Milton Keynes! They were accomplished choral singers, and showed members

Federation Chairman, Malvina Keech; National Chairman, Helen Carey; and Jeremy Spake.

flower arranging, paper-folding, how to dress in a kimono and the intricacies of the tea-making ceremony.

A County Supper was held at Yardley Hastings when Anthony Peddle, the paralympic gold medal winner and world record holding weightlifter inspired everyone with his quiet determination to get on with life despite the constraints of his disability. As this was held in the evening it was much appreciated by working members who had the opportunity to touch his Gold medal.

Members had the opportunity to visit the Dutch bulb fields in April and the Sundial Museum at Cambridge in May. Visits were made to all WIs, the main reason being to encourage them all to complete the Federation Survey. More trips were planned to Waddenham Manor in June, the Royal Show in July, the Globe Theatre in September as well as two longer excursions to the Wye Valley and to France centred on Arras. The final destination was the Royal School of Needlework in November.

The Intermediate General Meeting meant we had another overnight stay, this time just outside Cardiff so that we could arrive in time for the next day's proceedings. We managed to fit in in a visit to Shirley Valentine at the theatre the night before.

White water rafting was a new adventure for many, with Grow, Gather and Gain being held at Sulgrave and Wine, Words and Music at St. Andrew's Hospital.

The various walks around the county had been cancelled due to Foot and Mouth restrictions, but members would participate in the Car Treasure Hunt. Another Choir Day at Doddridge Memorial Centre, Northampton, would provide a fulfilling day for some whilst others decided the Annual Council Meeting at Spinney Hill Hall, was for them with National Chairman, Helen Carey visiting us and the guest speaker being Jeremy Spake.

We would scamper into 2002 with the same urge to travel and so were off to the RSC and Stratford upon Avon, a 4-day holiday to Rouen in France and an 8-day holiday to Ontario, Canada. We had two new vice-chairmen, Diana Birch, Yelvertoft, who was aleady doing a splendid job as Newsletter Editor, and Christine Farmer, Preston Capes, who was chairman of Combined Interests. Maureen Walton, remained as treasurer, whilst Diana Benarr had found it necessary to resign due to other commitments.

The Challenge Trophy for a WI Wallhanging was won by Hunsbury Hill, with Daventry runners- up. It was also a sad year as former VCOs had passed away, namely Mary Blackmore (Sparrow) Oakway, Joan Kerr, Gayton (formerly Moulton Afternoon), Christina Sergeant, Kelmarsh, Harrington & Arthingworth, and also two very talented craft members, Joan White, Weston Favell Village and Mary Pebody, Wootton.

The County Lunches had become a great success and there was much to learn from the distinguished speakers we had managed to engage to speak to members. In March we travelled to King's Sutton whee we heard Libby Foster, the niece of Dame Myra Hess, talk about her favourite aunt and all her achievements.

Hand sewn boxes were the subject of a one-day course at WI House in April, which brought back memories to me of going to the home of Mary Pebody where committee members learnt this art.

The WI takes you in all directions and we went to Brighton for the Intermediate General Meeting where we stayed overnight at the Hickstead Resort Hotel. One of our members, Gill Douglas, Ravensthorpe, attended a Lo-Salt Conference at Denman College and commented 'Never during my professional life have I heard so many speakers of such exceptional quality at one event'. Subjects covered were heart disease, stroke, hypertension, diet, nutrition and cancer, exercise, healthy eating for children, pre-prepared foods, the role of supermarkets, global inequality in food, supplements and additives.

Having received a bursary from the Federation to attend this course Gill was only too willing to talk to WIs to pass on all she had learnt.

An early Autumn visit to the Eden Project and the Lost Gardens of Heligan where entertainment was provided for us on one evening by the Cornwall Federation was followed by the Annual Council Meeting when Paul Whittaker talked about Music and the Deaf, having been totally deaf himself from the age of 8. The Challenge Trophy for a Golden Jubilee County Lunch was won by Hunsbury Hill after a final 'cook-off' at Denman College.

To get members into festivities mode a 4-day visit was made to Christmas Markets based in Valkenburg, Holland and in Cologne, Germany. Then came the Christmas Appetiser with Malcolm Tyler's choice of carols and music followed by the Brackley and District Brass Band, and of course mince pies and the Chairman's Punch. The final outing was a Theatre visit to Milton Keynes to see Buddy, the musical show based on Buddy Holly's life.

Sadly Sarah Harris, Easton & Collyweston, could no longer undertake the excellent covers she had produced for the Newsletter over the past three years so we were looking for a replacement. It was the Golden Jubilee of the Queen's Coronation and nationally there were 8,000 WIs, with Lady Brunner as chairman. At that time we had approximately 7,500 members, still being linked with the Soke of Peterborough. Lady Cynthia Spencer was President and Mrs. Roberta Lankester, East Haddon Chairman. Members refused that year to rafify the proposal that we should have a printed newsletter!

Two new WI Advisers joined the team, Diane Bradbury, Bugbrooke, and Mary Sheldon, Moulton Afternoon.

2003 found Malvina Keech in pensive mood and in her letter to members in January she reiterated the four main purposes of the WI and also published a Code of Conduct for Committee Members under the headings 'I agree to' and 'I hope to'. Many opportunities to learn new crafts were in the pipeline, for instance, patchwork bags, beaded bracelets, Victoran paper lace and sugar craft. Artists were encouraged with water colour classes and drawing with pastels. The more energetic tried fencing, darts and skittles, whilst those wishing to lead a gentler life entered the County Quiz or attended County Lunches. These were held at Weldon in March when the speaker was Joy Palmer giving her talk on being evacuated in World War II, and to Harlestone in September when the speaker was Michelle Leach who at that time was casting director of the well-known playwright Alan Ayckbourn.

Two former Chairmen died in 2003, Lady Brunner who had been

National Chairman from 1951 to 1956, and was the granddaughter of Sir Henry Irving, and Pauline Duff, Northamptonshire Chairman from 1971-1974. Both had worked tirelessly for the WI, but Pauline we knew as a great raconteur, a WI judge, a hard worker for the East of England Show, and someone who was always cheerful.

The National Federation had launched a Community Challenge competition. inviting WIs to think up different ways of helping in their communities. An Open House was held at Brixworth in April when representatives from all manner of local and national organisations talked about how they would like to work with WIs to make a difference in the communities around Northamptonshire. We were delighted to have National Vice -Chairman, Barbara Gill, of Leicester & Rutland with us on this occasion. The first challenge issued in the newsletter was the Lions Club suggestion for a 'bottle' in the fridge. The bottle contains a form with details of blood groups, medication being taken and where it is kept, allergies, medical condition, contacts, etc. and is recommended for being simple, not costing anything and taking up a small amount of space in the fridge, but above all 'it can save lives' This is particularly useful for the vulnerable, i.e. those who are alone, elderly or disabled. The outcome of this competition for new ideas was to be announced later in the year.

Walking was back on the agenda and we were out and about in Welford, Stoke Bruerne and along the Thames Valley. The not so energetic went on outings to Chester for a Taste of Europe weekend, to the Loire Valley and French Chateaux, to Southwell to see a Workhouse and the Minster and to Macclesfield to visit the Silk Museum.

The Annual Council Meeting on 29th October consisted of the talented duo of Susanne Collini (soprano) and Jennifer Partridge (piano) giving a highly entertaining account of the life and music of George Gershwin. The year ended with Northamptonshire members staging a display of what Northamptonshire members had achieved over 85 years, again at Brixworth, and then celebrating this with cheese and wine parties at Naseby, Islip, Chipping Warden and Kislingbury. We had great fun researching this and then trying to perform in Land Girl uniforms, County Chairman mode with hats, etc.

But there are two remaining items to conclude this history. One which has caused more publicity than one could have imagined, the other being more low key but both showing the organisation's ability to fund raise. The first is the Yorkshire Calendar which was prompted by the death of a WI husband and his wife and friends wishing to do

A La Calendar Girls 2003 – Mary Sheldon, Val Bellamy, Diana Birch, Christine Farmer, Malvina Keech and Jenny Hayes.

something to raise money for the Leukaemia Trust Fund. This calendar was made into a film and six of our Board of Trustees were invited to The World Premiere at the Odeon, Leicester Square. They obviously enjoyed this special occasion because the next time we see these members in on the cover of the newsletter and in the local press 'a la Calendar girls'. Who said the WI was not capable of having fun and, yes, having a laugh at its own expense from time to time.

The second item is that of our international work and what has been achieved over the past ten years, mostly under the direction of Susan Addams, Welton. Initially it was Anne Wright, Wappenham, who instigated the first ACWW project in Nepal to enlarge a school by the provision of four more classrooms providing basic primary education for children. The school also provided literacy classes for women after school and a training centre for teachers in school holidays. The cost was £2,136 and Northamptonshire's total donation was £1,805, the remainder of the cost being donated by another Federation.

Following this project during 1990–1992, members contributed to the Uganda Indigenous Women's Club based in Buwambo village.

This was to provide support for aid sufferers and their families and the funds raised were to enable them to become self-sufficient in their work through setting up a poultry income generation scheme. A target of £2,000 was agreed and a total of £2,009 was raised between 1994–6.

The Drinking Water project was to provide drinking water for a school for children, which also doubled as a training centre in agriculture for young women, and also to make this water available to the surrounding community. Again a target of £2,000 was agreed but the generous amount of £3,208 was achieved, helped by a collection of foreign coins. This was collected from 2000–2002 and finally from 2002–2004, although £2,000 was again agreed as the target amount, in fact £2,654.86 was raised for a Bore Well and Overhead Tank in Ottanthangal, India, to provide drinking water at a school for polio affected children.

Susan was the co-ordinator of most of these projects, as well as representing the Federation at ACWW Triennial Conferences all over the world – New Zealand, South Africa, Canada, Finland, etc. The Federation paid her registration fees, but fortunately Susan was able to travel with her retired husband and treat these occasions as holidays. She was also appointed to an ACWW sub- committee and at her last Triennial was the flag bearer, literally, for Great Britain, and must have felt very proud to carry out this task on behalf of all WI members.

In the early days WI programmes always had a motto for each month and so I cannot leave without quoting one from King's Sutton in 1922 – 'There is no study that is not capable of delighting us after a little application'. Lady Anglesey whose WI was the very first in Great Britain and the National Chairman I most admired said 'Tolerant and informed we must continue to be, apathetic we must not become, but our spread through a considerable cross-section of society gives us a special opportunity to be passionate for moderation, to hang on to rational argument and commonsense and work for the good of the whole community, all of which will require strenuous activity'.

APPENDIX

COUNTY PRESIDENTS
1920–1930   Lady Knightley, Badby
1931–1962   Countess Cynthia Spencer, Brington
1963–1969   Lady Catherine Macdonald-Buchanan, Cottesbrooke
1971–1991   Mrs. Mildred Cockram, Stoke Bruerne & Shutlanger

COUNTY CHAIRMEN
1918–1920   Miss Simpson, Chelveston
1921 Jan/Aug. Mrs. Lloyd, Brigstock
1922–1939   Miss Bouverie, Hardingstone
1939–1949   Mrs. Edith Renton, Guilsborough
1949–1951   Lady Catherine Macdonald-Buchanan, Cottesbrooke
1951–1954   Mrs. R. Lankester, East Haddon
1954–1957   Mrs. A. Cunnington, Long Buckby
1957–1960   The Hon. Mrs. E.C. Capron, Southwick
1960–1964   Mrs. Ethelwyn Tynan, Islip
1964–1965   Mrs. Dorothy Davidson, Grendon
1965–1968   Mrs. Philip L. Battle, Hackleton & District
1968–1971   Mrs. D.S. Cockram, Stoke Bruerne & Shutlanger
1971–1974   Mrs. J.H. Duff, Scaldwell
1974–1977   Mrs. D.W. Bowler, Mears Ashby
1977–1980   Mrs. G.A.H. Palfreyman, Maidwell &District
1980–1983   Mrs. N.L. Walker, Grendon & Easton Maudit
1983–1987   Mrs. C.T. Haynes, Ashley with Weston-by-Welland Dingley & Brampton Ash
1987–1990   Mrs. Caroline Raven, Lois Weedon & Weston
1990–1992   Mrs. W. Shurville, Weston Favell
1992–1995   Mrs. Sue Bird, Easton & Collyweston
1995–1997   Mrs. Sue Tait, Cottesbrooke
1997–2000   Mrs. Christine Farmer, Preston Capes
2000–2003   Mrs. Malvina Keech, Cranford
2003–   Mrs. Diana Birch, Yelvertoft

COUNTY TREASURERS
1918–1919   Miss Mary Bouverie, Hardingstone
1920–1922   Mrs. E.M. Barker, Earls Barton
1923–1950   Mrs. Millicent Eunson

1951–1956   Mrs. Edna Clarke
1957–1959   Mrs. Holt, Elton
1959–1962   Mrs. Joan Battle, The Bramptons
1963–1985   Miss Margaret Aspinal, Overstone & Sywell
1985–1986   Mrs. Beryl Oldrey, Hackleton
1986–1988   Mrs. Liz Fox, Barnwell
1988–1991   Mrs. Winnie Shurville, Weston Favell
1991–1994   Mrs. Malvina Keech, Cranford
1994–1996   Mrs. Sue Tait, Cottesbrooke
1996–1999   Mrs. Reta Evans, Aston-le-Walls & Appletree
1999–2003   Mrs. Maureen Walton, The Bramptons
2003–   Mrs. Christine Farmer, Preston Capes

COUNTY SECRETARIES

1918–1945   Mrs. E.M. Barker, Moulton
1945–1946   Miss Law
1947–1956   Miss Berridge
1957–1959   Miss E.M. Whatley
1960–1976   Mrs. Mary Perry
1977–1991   Mrs. Kathleen Pinton
1991–1997   Mrs. Anne Pooley
1998   Mrs. Brenda Orchard
1998–   Miss Margaret Foster

COUNTY OFFICES

1918   Rest Room, Depot
       The Parade, Northampton
1926   Abington Street
1929   Raleigh Chambers, St. Giles Terrace
1936   33 Marefair
1958   11 Albion Place

WIs transferred to HUNTS & PETERBOROUGH FEDERATION

BARNACK, CASTER & AILSWORTH, EYE, GLINTON, MARHOLM, MAXEY, NEWARD, NEWBOROUGH & BOROUGH FEN, NORTHBOROUGH, PEAKIRK, WERRINGTON and WITTERING

SOURCES OF INFORMATION

I acknowledge with grateful thanks permission to quote from a wide range of publications, but particular thanks are due to Northamptonshire members who have provided potted histories. Without the help of all the following it would not have been possible to complete such a comprehensive history of the women's institutes in Northamptonshire.

Awards for All, East Midlands:
Grant to enable us to get project started, ie, recording of archives and lodging with Northamptonshire Record Society.

Northamptonshire Newspapers:
Editions of former papers, CHRONICLE, ECHO, MERCURY, HERALD, INDEPENDENT, NORTHAMPTONSHIRE LIFE.

National Federation of Women's Institutes:
Home & Country magazines
Robertson Scott, J.W., *The Story of the Women's Institute Movement*, The Village Press 1925
Davies, Constance, *A Grain of Mustard Seed*, 1953
Jenkins, Inez, *The History of the Women's Institute Movement of England and Wales 1953*
McCall, Cicely, *Our Villages*, 1956
Parris Carola, *Denman College*, 1973
Goodenough, Simon, *Jam and Jerusalem*, 1977
Garner, Gwen, *Extraordinary Women*, 1995
Stamper, Anne, *Rooms off the Corridor*, 1998

Associated Countrywomen of the World:
Working with Women Worldwide, Highlights of 75 years of ACWW 2004, 24 Tufton Street, London SW1P 2RB
Addams, Susan, NCFWI, Information of Northamptonshire Projects

Northamptonshire County Federation of Women's Institutes: Minute Books, Annual Reports, Round-Up, Northamptonshire WI News, A County Miscellany, Village Voices, Within Living Memory.